Introduction

The counting of the Omer, which spans the forty-nine days from Passover to Shavuot, stems from the biblical commandment to harvest the first sheaf of barley on the second day of Passover, and then to offer bread of the wheat harvest on Shavuot. In between these two grain-offerings are forty-nine days, and there is a biblical commandment to count each of these forty-nine days. After the destruction of the Temple, the command became simply to count the days sequentially: Today is one day of the Omer, today is two days of the Omer… today is one week and one day, that is eight days of the Omer, and so forth. The seven weeks of the Omer represent a process of completion: the first sheaf of grain becomes a full loaf of bread. So too, the liberation of Passover flowers into the giving of Torah at Shavuot.

The story of the Omer begins with Passover, the liberation from Egypt. Women are prominent in that story, from the midwives who saved Hebrew babies, to Miriam who watched over the infant Moses in the Nile, to Tziporah who saved Moses from the Angel of Death. The story of the Omer ends with the wheat harvest, when Ruth the Moabite went down to the threshing floor to ask Boaz to create new life with her. The birth, growth and harvest of seed from the earth is a process intertwined with the lives of women and with the Shekhinah, the Divine Presence who is embodied in the life-force of the world.

This Omer calendar offers the story of one biblical woman for each of the forty-nine days of the omer. It is meant both to teach about the women of the Bible and to honor the Shekhinah at the season of harvest. My prayer is that this calendar will help everyone to recognize the Shekhinah working in their lives.

The Omer and the Sefirot

Over time the Omer became a period of mourning because of tragedies that occurred during that time, including the death of many of the talmudic sage Rabbi Akiva's students. Later, mystics saw the Omer period as a time to honor the different attributes of God. Jewish mystics imagined God as having ten faces or attributes called *sefirot*, including *chesed* (love or expansiveness), *gevurah* (strength, severity, or judgment), *tiferet* (beauty, balance or compassion), and so forth.

The mythic characters of the Bible represent these attributes — for example, Abraham represents *chesed*, Moses and Aaron represent *netzach* and *hod*, while Rachel represents *malchut* (the indwelling feminine face of God called Shekhinah). Kabbalists have come to see the counting of the Omer as a way to meditate on seven of the *sefirot* and include them in one's own life.

The seven *sefirot* of the Omer are:

- חסד *Chesed*: love, lovingkindness, generosity or expansiveness. *Chesed* is the outpouring of love into the universe.

- גבורה *Gevurah*: strength, rigor, severity, judgment or limitation. *Gevurah* represents justice, discipline, boundary-making, and severity.

- תפארת *Tiferet*: compassion, beauty, balance, truth. The combination of *chesed* and *gevurah*, *tiferet* represents the ability to mix expansive and limiting forces and achieve harmony.

- נצח *Netzach*: endurance, victory, or persistence. *Netzach* (connected with prophecy) is an expansive force that survives, acts on the world, and gets things done.

- הוד *Hod*: glory, humility, gratitude or receptivity. *Hod* (connected with priesthood) opens itself to receive from the Divine, and shapes what is received with gratitude, openness, and humility.

- יסוד *Yesod*: Connectivity, intimacy, or foundation. *Yesod* is the generative foundation of the universe, and represents connection, communication, and sexuality.

- מלכות *Malkhut*: Royalty, dignity, majesty, or wholeness. *Malkhut* is the unity of all, and also represents the majesty of the Divine presence, the Shekhinah.

Each of the weeks of the Omer represents one of these seven attributes. Each day within a week represents a combination of that week's attribute with another one. For example, the first week of the Omer represents *chesed*. The first day is *chesed shebechesed* (love within love), while the second day is *gevurah shebechesed* (strength within love) and the third is *tiferet shebechesed* (compassion within love) and so forth.

The eighth day begins the second week, the week of *gevurah*, and the first day of that week is *chesed shebegevurah*, love within strength. The cycle continues onward through the weeks until the last week, which represents *malchut* — the forty-third day of the Omer is *chesed shebemalchut*, the forty-fourth is *gevurah shebemalchut*, and the final forty-ninth day is *malchut shebemalchut*.

The traditional kabbalistic system assigns male biblical characters to the *sefirot*, but not many female characters. Yet each of us embodies the Divine in a unique way. The women in this calendar were chosen to correspond to the kabbalistic attributes of the Omer and to invite us to meditate on and embody these ethical characteristics in our own lives.

How to Count the Omer

We count the day of the Omer at night, saying a blessing before we count. If one forgets to count at night, one counts during the day without a blessing, and continues the count the next evening, including the blessing. If one forgets during an entire twenty-four hour period, the tradition is to continue the count on the following days, but without the blessing.

The blessings on the inside back cover include a traditional option with male God-language, and also a creative blessing for those who wish to use female God-language.

History of this Project

Rabbi Jill Hammer first wrote the *Omer Calendar of Biblical Women* in 2003 for the use of Ma'yan: The Jewish Women's Project at the JCC of Manhattan and appeared on ritualwell.org. It was disseminated by e-mail to many of Ma'yan's friends and supporters, and was featured in the JCC lobby during the Omer season. Many thanks to Eve Landau and the women of Ma'yan for their support of the Omer Calendar of Biblical Women. The copyright for the text of both the original Omer Calendar of Biblical Women and this revised version is retained by Jill Hammer.

Week One: *Chesed*

Love/Generosity/Abundance

Misés e Jocabed, Pedro Américo, 1884
See page 11

1. Shekhinah

Chesed shebeChesed   Love within Love

בכל אתר דישראל גלו תמן שכינתא אתגליא עמהון

"In every place to which Israel was exiled, the Shekhinah went with them."
—Zohar, *Parashat Shemot*

The first day of the Omer is the second day of Passover, when the Israelites begin their journey out of Egypt and through the desert. Jeremiah calls to Israel: "I remember for you the *chesed* of your youth, the love of your bridal days, how you followed me in the wilderness, in a land unsown." Jeremiah depicts the newborn holy community as a bride, following God through the wilderness toward Mount Sinai.

For kabbalists, the community of the Hebrews is an embodiment of Shekhinah, the feminine presence of the divine. The Shekhinah dwells within them and also hovers above them embodied in the clouds of glory. She gives Israel manna to eat and water to drink. On Shavuot, the Shekhinah appears on Mount Sinai, embodied in the Torah. The Zohar imagines Her pushing and shoving her way through crowds of angels in order to come down to earth and be with human beings.

The Shekhinah is the channel for all blessings — though she can also be a terrifying figure with spears and meteors for hair. Throughout history Shekhinah is Israel's defender and nurturer, hovering over them when they pray and accompanying them when they go into exile. Shekhinah appears for them in the renewal of the new moon, in the study of Torah, in the peace of the Sabbath. We emulate the Divine Presence by feeding, clothing, and sheltering others, and becoming channels of blessing into the world.

Hayom yom echad la'omer.
Today is the first day of the Omer.

2. Miriam
Exodus 2, 15:20-21, Numbers 12, 20:1-13

Gevurah shebeChesed   Strength within Love

וַתִּקַּח מִרְיָם הַנְּבִיאָה אֲחוֹת אַהֲרֹן אֶת־הַתֹּף בְּיָדָהּ וַתֵּצֶאןָ כָל־הַנָּשִׁים אַחֲרֶיהָ בְּתֻפִּים
וּבִמְחֹלֹת: וַתַּעַן לָהֶם מִרְיָם שִׁירוּ לַיהוָה כִּי־גָאֹה גָּאָה סוּס וְרֹכְבוֹ רָמָה בַיָּם:

"Miriam the prophetess, sister of Aaron, took a drum in her hand, and all the women went out after her with drums and dances. Miriam sang to them: "Sing to the Adonai, who has triumphed mightily, and thrown horse and rider into the sea!" —Exodus 15:20-21

As a girl, Miriam watches over her brother Moses on the shore of the Nile. She dares to convince an Egyptian princess to save her brother. In a midrash, Miriam is a midwife to the Hebrews, and defies Pharaoh in order to save innocent male babies. Miriam is an agent of *chesed*, love, in the world — but throughout Miriam's life, love requires great courage and strength. She crosses the sea to freedom and raises her voice in song even while the sea is crashing down on the Egyptians — *chesed* and *gevurah* together. Legend holds that a well of water follows Miriam in the desert so that all may drink from it.

Later in her life, Miriam criticizes Moses for not honoring her leadership of the people. God punishes her with skin disease and exile—this may be a story about how women are exiled from the ranks of priests and leaders. Miriam spends seven days and nights outside the camp, alone in the desert sun and chill darkness, until she is healed and readmitted. Miriam's chesed, her poured-out gifts, are limited by *gevurah*, by the boundaries of her world. Miriam dies in the wilderness, and her well disappears, but the mystics tell us that in every generation it returns to her people to heal them. When we imitate Miriam, we know that to love well we must love with courage. When we do this, we know our love will last and return.

Hayom shnei yamim la'omer.
Today is the second day of the Omer.

3. The Attendant to Naaman's Wife
II Kings 5

Tiferet shebeChesed   Compassion within Love

וַאֲרָם יָצְאוּ גְדוּדִים וַיִּשְׁבּוּ מֵאֶרֶץ יִשְׂרָאֵל נַעֲרָה קְטַנָּה וַתְּהִי לִפְנֵי אֵשֶׁת נַעֲמָן׃

"The Arameans went out raiding, and they took captive from the land of Israel a little girl, and she served before the wife of Naaman." —II Kings 5:2

Some characters in the Bible pass so fleetingly that we almost miss them, like a certain young servant girl. In the book of Kings, during the period when Israel is divided into two kingdoms, an Israelite girl is captured as a slave and made to serve the wife of an Aramean commander. The enemy commander, like Miriam, is afflicted with a skin condition. The Israelite girl knows of the prophet Elisha, who can perform miracles. She says to her mistress: "I wish Master could come before the prophet in Samaria and be healed!" This child shows compassion even for a man who has enslaved her and made war on her people.

The commander, Naaman, takes the little girl seriously and goes to the prophet Elisha. Elisha orders him to bathe in the river. At first, Naaman refuses, but eventually he does what Elisha suggests and is cured. He also becomes a believer in the Israelite God. One can hope (although the text does not say so) that Naaman shows his gratitude by freeing his loving and compassionate slave. We can adopt Naaman's servant into our lives when we use deep wellsprings of love to speak in compassion even to those who have hurt us.

Hayom shlosha yamim la'omer.
Today is the third day of the Omer.

4. Yocheved
Exodus 2

Netzach shebeChesed   Endurance within Love

וַתַּהַר הָאִשָּׁה וַתֵּלֶד בֵּן וַתֵּרֶא אֹתוֹ כִּי־טוֹב הוּא וַתִּצְפְּנֵהוּ שְׁלֹשָׁה יְרָחִים:
וְלֹא־יָכְלָה עוֹד הַצְּפִינוֹ וַתִּקַּח־לוֹ תֵּבַת גֹּמֶא וַתַּחְמְרָה בַחֵמָר וּבַזָּפֶת...

"The woman conceived and bore a son, and when she saw how beautiful she was, she hid him for three months. When she could not hide him anymore, she took a wicker basket for him and caulked it with bitumen and pitch…" —Exodus 2:2-3

It is the time of Pharaoh's decree that all boys born to Hebrew women must be thrown into the Nile. Yocheved loves her newborn son so much that she is willing to take extraordinary action to hide him. She keeps him in the house for three months. When she can no longer endanger her family by hiding an infant, she weaves a basket and sets the baby boy afloat in the Nile. (See artist's interpretation on page 6.) Yocheved's love leads her to the quality of *netzach* — decisive action, and faith that she can overcome any obstacle.

A few hours later, Miriam calls Yocheved to the riverbank. An Egyptian princess hands Yocheved her baby back, and tells her to nurse the child until he is older, when he will be brought to the palace and raised as a prince. Imagine the astonishment and triumph of that moment! This is *netzach shebechesed* — how love creates extraordinary possibilities.

Yocheved's love births and nurtures three children whom the prophet Micah calls "three leaders of Israel"— Moses, Aaron, and Miriam. Yocheved is the engine of the future. A midrash says that Yocheved lived to see the Exodus — her son Moses as redeemer, her son Aaron as high priest, her daughter Miriam dancing by the sea. We are most like Yocheved when we act for the sake of love, when we move heaven and earth to give our love to others.

Hayom arba'ah yamim la'omer.
Today is the fourth day of the Omer.

5. The Mother in Solomon's Trial
I Kings 3

Hod shebeChesed   Surrender within Love

וַתֹּאמֶר הָאִשָּׁה אֲשֶׁר־בְּנָהּ הַחַי אֶל־הַמֶּלֶךְ כִּי־נִכְמְרוּ רַחֲמֶיהָ עַל־בְּנָהּ
וַתֹּאמֶר ׀ בִּי אֲדֹנִי תְּנוּ־לָהּ אֶת־הַיָּלוּד הַחַי וְהָמֵת אַל־תְּמִיתֻהוּ
וְזֹאת אֹמֶרֶת גַּם־לִי גַם־לָךְ לֹא יִהְיֶה גְּזֹרוּ׃

"The woman whose son was the living one pleaded with the king… she said, 'Please, my lord, give her the living child, don't kill it!" —I Kings 3:26

King Solomon is known throughout the land for his justice and wisdom. Two women, prostitutes, bring a case before him. One woman tells him that she has borne a child, and the woman living with her also bore a child. "During the night this woman lay on her child and it died. She got up in the middle of the night and took my son from my side while I was sleeping, and laid him in her bosom, and she laid her dead son in my bosom."

The other woman denies the story, saying that the living child is hers. Solomon orders a sword to be brought. He proclaims that both the dead child and the living one shall be divided with half of each child given to each mother. One woman — it's not clear who — cries, "Give her the live child, and do not kill it!" The other woman callously insists, "The child shall be neither mine nor yours; divide it." Solomon declares that the live child shall be given to the woman who was willing to give it up, "for she is its mother."

Hod, glory, is sometimes explained as "surrender" or "yielding." The mother in this story surrenders her child so that it may live. We act in her spirit when we act in the true best interest of those we love, even when that is most difficult. The woman Solomon judges reveals the inner depths of *hod shebechesed* — yielding out of love.

Hayom chamisha yamim la'omer.
Today is the fifth day of the Omer.

6. Serach bat Asher
Genesis 46:17, Numbers 26:46, I Chronicles 7:30

Yesod shebeChesed   Connection within Love

וּבְנֵי אָשֵׁר יִמְנָה וְיִשְׁוָה וְיִשְׁוִי וּבְרִיעָה וְשֶׂרַח אֲחֹתָם...

"Asher's sons were Imnah, Ishvah, Ishvi, and Beriah,
and their sister Serach." —Genesis 46:17

Serach is mentioned in a few genealogical lists as the daughter of Jacob's son Asher. One legend tells that when the brothers of Joseph learned that Joseph was alive, they were afraid the news would kill their aging father. They asked the wise Serach to tell Jacob. Serach sang the news to Jacob in rhyme while he was praying, awakening the spirit of God in him and allowing him to absorb the news. Jacob exclaimed: "May the mouth that told me these words never taste death!" And so Serach lives forever.

Serach confirmed for the Israelites that Moses was their redeemer, by remembering the "code words" of redemption that her father had taught her. Serach showed Moses where to find Joseph's bones, for the Israelites had promised to carry those bones out of Egypt when they were redeemed. Serach's love, her *chesed*, showed itself through *yesod* — through connecting one generation to another.

Today is the seventh day of Passover, the day on which we celebrate the crossing of the Sea of Reeds. There is a legend that in the time of the Talmud, Serach poked her head in the window of a study hall and told the Talmudic rabbis that the walls of the Sea looked like clear mirrors. Some say the Israelites saw in those mirrors all the generations of Israel, past and future. We are most like Serach when we show our love to the generations before and after us, by preserving memory and keeping stories alive.

Hayom shisha yamim la'omer.
Today is the sixth day of the Omer.

7. The Shunnamite
II Kings 4:8-37

Malchut shebeChesed   Majesty within Love

וַיְהִי הַיּוֹם וַיַּעֲבֹר אֱלִישָׁע אֶל־שׁוּנֵם וְשָׁם אִשָּׁה גְדוֹלָה וַתַּחֲזֶק־בּוֹ לֶאֱכָל־לָחֶם וַיְהִי מִדֵּי עָבְרוֹ יָסֻר שָׁמָּה לֶאֱכָל־לָחֶם:

"One day Elisha passed through Shunem.
A great woman lived there, and she invited him to eat a meal…" —II Kings 4:8

The Shunammite (a woman of the town of Shunem) is a wealthy married woman living in the time of the kings of Israel and Judah. The Shunammite suggests to her husband that they build the prophet Elisha a chamber on their roof so that he has somewhere to stay when he travels. Elisha asks how he can help her, but her regal reply is: "I live among my own people." I want for nothing, she implies. She does lovingkindness out of a sense of abundance and majesty: *chesed shebemalkhut*.

Elisha knows that the Shunammite has no child. He prays for her to become pregnant. The child grows older, but one day he is out in the field with his father and he develops sunstroke. He runs back to his mother and dies on her lap. Without a word to her husband, the Shunammite rides to the prophet. She bows before him, yet she does not plead for her child. She only says: "Did I desire a child of my lord? Did I not say to you: "Don't delude me?" Elisha goes to the home of the Shunammite and lies face down upon the child "with his mouth on its mouth, his eyes on its eyes, his hands on its hands" until it revives. Without a word, the Shunammite bows, takes up her child, and departs.

The Shunammite has great *chesed*: she is kind to the prophet, loves her son deeply, and cares for her husband. Yet her *chesed* is always full of *malkhut*, majesty. She helps others, relies on herself, and when she needs help she asks for it with dignity. We are most like the Shunammite when we give and receive love gracefully.

Hayom shivah yamim, she heim shvua echad la'omer.
Today is seven days, one full week, of the Omer.

Week Two: *Gevurah*
Strength/Judgment/Severity/Harshness

Lot's Wife, Janet Shafner, 1996
See page 20

8. Chava
Eve, the first woman (Genesis 2-4)

Chesed shebeGevurah   Love within Strength

וַיִּקְרָא הָאָדָם שֵׁם אִשְׁתּוֹ חַוָּה כִּי הִוא הָיְתָה אֵם כָּל־חָי:

"The man called the name of his woman Eve, for she was the mother of all life."
—Genesis 3:20

Eve is a newborn creature dwelling in a perfect garden full of fruits of all kind. She and her male partner Adam have been limited in a single way: they are forbidden to eat the fruit of the tree of knowledge of good and evil. Eve disobeys God and eats the forbidden fruit, and she and Adam must go into exile. The fruit Eve picks gives her the bitterness of death, but it also gives her wisdom and self-knowledge. All the humans that ever come to exist, come to exist because of Eve's decision to disobey God. Out of the gevurah, the judgment, that God decrees comes the chesed, the ongoing expansion of all the generations that descend from Adam and Eve.

Eve's first-born son Cain murders her second son Abel. Yet she does not give up the potential for love; she goes on to have another child, and names him Seth (Shet), meaning foundation or gift. She feels love and gratitude in spite of what she has suffered. Maybe she has a glimmer of all the love — and all the pain — that she has begun by initiating human history. *Chesed shebegevurah* is the knowledge that within the finitude of our lives there can still be love. We are most like Eve when we acknowledge the pain of our circumstances, and still remain open to the possibility of love, work, and wonder.

Hayom shmonah yamim, sheheim shvua echad veyom echad la'omer.
Today is eight days, one week and one day, of the Omer.

9. Vashti
Esther 1

Gevurah shebeGevurah Strength within Strength

כִּי־יֵצֵא דְבַר־הַמַּלְכָּה עַל־כָּל־הַנָּשִׁים לְהַבְזוֹת בַּעְלֵיהֶן בְּעֵינֵיהֶן בְּאָמְרָם הַמֶּלֶךְ אֲחַשְׁוֵרוֹשׁ אָמַר לְהָבִיא אֶת־וַשְׁתִּי הַמַּלְכָּה לְפָנָיו וְלֹא־בָאָה:

"King Ahasuerus commanded that Queen Vashti be brought before him, but she did not come." —Esther 1:17

Vashti is the queen of Persia. She and her husband Ahasuerus throw separate feasts: he hosts one for the men, and she makes one for the women. The king's feast becomes drunk and rowdy. The king orders Vashti to come and dance before him and his guests. One legend says that he wants her to dance wearing only her royal crown!

Out of pride, modesty, or discretion, Vashti refuses the king's request. The king deposes her, and the stage is set for a Jewish girl named Esther to become queen and save her people. Vashti disappears from the story—whether because she is executed, exiled, or simply engulfed by the walls of the harem. The king then legislates that all women obey their husbands. He is afraid of the power of a wife who disagrees with her spouse.

Vashti demonstrates the full meaning of *gevurah* — strength, justice, and the willingness to impose limits. She is strength within strength, the inner will that allows us to make the right decisions even when they are unpopular. We are most like Vashti when we know how to say "no" to something that hurts or degrades us or someone else, when we are willing to impose limits on ourselves and those around us in order to increase justice in the world.

Hayom tishah yamim, sheheim shvua echad ushnei yamim la'omer.
Today is nine days, one week and two days, of the Omer.

10. Idit
Lot's wife (Genesis 19)

Tiferet shebeGevurah   Severity within Compassion

וַתַּבֵּט אִשְׁתּוֹ מֵאַחֲרָיו וַתְּהִי נְצִיב מֶלַח:

"Lot's wife looked behind, and she became a pillar of salt." —Genesis 19:26

Abraham's nephew, Lot, lives with his wife in the city of Sodom. They have four daughters: two are married, and two still live at home. Sodom is rich and fertile, but known for its evil ways. God decides to destroy Sodom, and sends two angels to save Lot and his family. A mob gathers around Lot's house, threatening to sexually attack the angels. Lot offers his two virgin daughters to the mob as a substitute. The angels save the girls, and demand that Lot and his family leave the city without looking back. Lot tries to convince his sons-in-law to come with him, but they refuse. As Lot, his wife, and his two remaining daughters leave Sodom, Lot's wife looks back toward the burning city and is turned into a pillar of salt. (See artist's interpretation on page 16.)

Why does Lot's wife turn to salt? Pirkei DeRabbi Eliezer, an ancient midrash, suggests that she could not bear to leave her two married daughters to be destroyed in Sodom. She looked back in order to see if they were following her. Her looking back was not an act of disobedience but of compassion. Rabbi Cynthia A. Culpepper in *The Women's Torah Commentary* adds that in the Bible, a pillar is often a memorial. Lot's wife makes herself a memorial pillar to her daughters who have died. The midrashic name given to Lot's wife is Idit, which means witness. Idit turns back and shares the suffering of her daughters in Sodom. We bring Idit into our lives when we have the courage, *gevurah*, to have compassion, *tiferet*, and involve ourselves deeply in the pain of others.

Hayom asarah yamim, sheheim shvua echad ushloshah yamim la'omer.
Today is ten days, one week and three days, of the Omer.

11. Dinah
Genesis 30:21; 34

Netzach shebeGevurah   Enduring within Strength

וַתֵּצֵא דִינָה בַת־לֵאָה אֲשֶׁר יָלְדָה לְיַעֲקֹב לִרְאוֹת בִּבְנוֹת הָאָרֶץ:

"Dinah the daughter of Leah, whom Leah had borne to Jacob, went out to see the daughters of the land." —Genesis 34:1

Dinah is daughter of Jacob, Leah's last child and only girl. Her name means "judgment." Dinah is born into a world of limitation, of *gevurah*, simply because she is a girl. When she grows up and goes out to meet the other women of the region, a local prince rapes her. Her brothers slaughter an entire town to avenge her rape. Or, some say, Dinah finds a lover from a foreign tribe; her brothers call it a rape and kill her lover and his people to erase their shame. One ancient midrash even suggests that Dinah bears a daughter as a result of the rape, and her family forces her to give up the child (see Asnat, day 19).

Dinah lives in a world of *gevurah*. The Bible does not give her a voice to tell of her experience, nor does it tell us what becomes of her, as if the rape is the most important fact of her life. Yet Dinah has captured the imagination of modern storytellers. In Anita Diamant's *The Red Tent*, Dinah runs away and becomes a midwife in Egypt. In Deena Metzger's *What Dinah Thought*, Dinah speaks through the voice of a modern woman in search of her identity. One book about modern Jewish women is titled *The Tribe of Dinah*. Though Jacob gives Dinah no blessing and Moses gives her descendants no tribe, our generation can give Dinah a voice. For this reason, Dinah is *netzach shebegevurah* — endurance in spite of judgment. Her spirit endures and reminds us to reclaim the stories of the nameless and voiceless.

Hayom achad-asar yom, sheheim shvua echad ve'arba'ah yamim la'omer.
Today is eleven days, one week and four days, of the Omer.

12. Yemima, Ketziah, and Keren-happuch
Job's daughters (Job 42:14-15)

Hod shebeGevurah   Glory within Severity

וְלֹא נִמְצָא נָשִׁים יָפוֹת כִּבְנוֹת אִיּוֹב בְּכָל־הָאָרֶץ וַיִּתֵּן לָהֶם אֲבִיהֶם נַחֲלָה בְּתוֹךְ אֲחֵיהֶם׃

> "There were no women as beautiful as Job's daughters to be found in all the land. Their father gave them a land-inheritance alongside their brothers." —Job 42:15

Job, a righteous man, endures troubles he cannot bear, including the loss of his seven sons and three daughters. He cries out to God, demanding to know the reason for his suffering. Finally, God answers, telling Job only that God's knowledge and might are too great for Job to understand.

Yet because of Job's questioning, God rewards him with riches and health—as well as seven new sons and three new daughters. The seven new sons do not have names, but the three new daughters do. They are called Yemima (Bright Day), Ketziah (Cassia Tree), and Keren-happuch (Horn [container] of Eyeshadow). Unlike other daughters in the Bible, who have no inheritance if they have brothers, Yemima, Ketziah, and Keren-happuch receive land from their father equally with their brothers.

While surely these daughters cannot replace Job's daughters who died, they are a sign that hope is possible. Their receiving the gift of land from their father is a call to plant and nurture life, and it allows them to be independent actors able to pursue their own destinies. They represent the openness and beauty of hod even within the limitations of *gevurah*. We are most like Yemima, Ketziah, and Keren-happuch when we are able to begin again after tragedy, accepting that we can grow in spite of our brokenness.

This day of the Omer is *Yom haShoah*, Holocaust Memorial Day. It is appropriate to remember both victims of undeserved suffering and the new lives survivors have been able to build.

Hayom shneym-asar yom, sheheim shvua echad vechamishah yamim la'omer.
    Today is twelve days, one week and five days, of the Omer.

13. She'ilah
Bat Yiftach/Jephthah's daughter (Judges 11:34)

Yesod shebeGevurah   Connectivity Within Harshness

וַיִּקְרָא שֵׁם־הָאַחַת יְמִימָה וְשֵׁם הַשֵּׁנִית קְצִיעָה וְשֵׁם הַשְּׁלִישִׁית קֶרֶן הַפּוּךְ׃
וְלֹא נִמְצָא נָשִׁים יָפוֹת כִּבְנוֹת אִיּוֹב בְּכָל־הָאָרֶץ וַיִּתֵּן לָהֶם אֲבִיהֶם נַחֲלָה בְּתוֹךְ אֲחֵיהֶם׃

"When Yiftach came to his house in Mitzpah,
there was his daug*hter co*ming out to greet him with drums and with dances.
She was an only daughter; he had no son or daughter beside her." —Judges 11:34

Jephthah, a judge of Israel, is eager to win a battle against his enemies. He promises that he will sacrifice to God the first creature that comes from his doorway to greet him when he arrives home after the battle. But the one who greets him at his doorway is his daughter, dancing and playing the timbrel to celebrate his victory. "You have become my troubler!" Jephthah wails at her, failing to acknowledge that it is he, her father, who has become her troubler. Jephthah's daughter extracts a promise from her father that she may go to the hills for three months to mourn with her friends. Even after she is sacrificed (murdered), her friends continue to gather for four days in the year to sing songs in memory of her.

The rabbis of the Talmud name Jephthah's daughter She'ilah (questioner). They depict her as a learned woman who makes many arguments as to why she should be saved, all to no avail. Yet even in the midst of the severity, the *gevurah*, of her fate, she reaches out to friends who understand the pain she feels. These friends establish a festival in her memory. She'ilah represents *yesod shebegevurah* — in spite of her own pain she is able to connect with others and create relationships that surpass the limitations of her own life. We can remember She'ilah in our own lives when we establish families and friendships that remain strong even in harsh times.

Hayom shloshah-asar yom, sheheim shvua echad veshishah yamim la'omer.
Today is twelve days, one week and five days, of the Omer.

14. Leah
Genesis 29-32

Malchut shebeGevurah   Majesty within Strength

וַיָּבֹא יִפְתָּח הַמִּצְפָּה אֶל־בֵּיתוֹ וְהִנֵּה בִתּוֹ יֹצֵאת לִקְרָאתוֹ בְתֻפִּים וּבִמְחֹלוֹת
וְרַק הִיא יְחִידָה אֵין־לוֹ מִמֶּנּוּ בֵּן אוֹ־בַת:

"The Divine saw that Leah was unloved, and opened her womb…" —Genesis 29:31

Leah is the elder of two daughters of Laban, an Aramean owner of flocks and herds. Her younger sister Rachel is more beautiful than she— Rachel is lovely of form and appearance, while Leah has soft, weak eyes. The young shepherd Jacob, sent by his mother Rebekah (Laban's sister), to find a bride, falls in love with Rachel and serves seven years as payment for her hand. On their wedding night, Laban tricks Jacob and substitutes Leah as the bride. Jacob is outraged and demands Ra*chel* as well, but the deed is done. *Leah* remains Jacob's wife.

As Leah bears children, she names them and expresses through the names her desire for Jacob to love her. Her first son is Reuven, "behold a son"— "The Lord has seen my affliction; now my husband will love me." Her second son is Shimon: "God heard that I was hated." Yet as Leah grows older, she finds some contentment in her own life — her fourth son is called Judah, "praise." Leah becomes, in the words of a traditional midrash, "a master of praise," one who is gifted at thanksgiving.

In the Zohar, Leah represents the "upper mother," *Binah*, the divine womb from which life and understanding flow. She represents *malkhut shebegevurah*, majesty within strength, because in spite of the painful reality of living with a jealous sister and a man who does not love her, Leah finds the dignity of praise and gratitude. We are most like Leah when we are able to live not only for those we want to love us, but for ourselves and for God.

Hayom arba'ah-asar yom, sheheim shnei shavuot la'omer.
Today is fourteen days, two weeks of the Omer.

Week Three: *Tiferet*
Compassion/Balance/Truth

The Finding of Moses, Sir Lawrence Alma-Tadema, 1904
See page 33

15. Shifrah and Puah
Exodus 1

Chesed shebeTiferet   Love within Compassion

וַתִּירֶאןָ הַמְיַלְּדֹת אֶת־הָאֱלֹהִים וְלֹא עָשׂוּ כַּאֲשֶׁר דִּבֶּר אֲלֵיהֶן מֶלֶךְ מִצְרָיִם וַתְּחַיֶּיןָ אֶת־הַיְלָדִים:

"The midwives feared God, and they did not do as the king of Egypt had commanded them; they let the children live." —Exodus 1:17

Shifrah and Puah, two hardworking midwives, help Hebrew slaves deliver babies in the land of Egypt. Pharaoh summons them and commands them to kill every Hebrew baby boy they deliver, while letting the girls live. Yet Shifrah and Puah show compassion to the Hebrew mothers and their children, and do not obey the king's command.

When Pharaoh summons the midwives again and demands to know why they have not carried out his order, Shifrah and Puah use his own prejudices against him. They claim: "The Hebrew women are like animals. Before the midwife can come to them, they give birth." The Hebrew word for "animals" (*chayot*) can also mean "alive"—the midwives hint that the Hebrew women are living beings who deserve respect.

God rewards Shifrah and Puah — "God built them houses." This may mean many children or lasting family dynasties. Or, one interpretation of this verse is that God made schools of midwifery for them so that they could pass on their heroic values!

Some legends say that Shifrah and Puah are Yocheved and Miriam, the mother and sister of Moses. Others imagine Shifrah and Puah as Egyptian women who act to preserve the lives of others because it is the right thing to do. Shifrah and Puah show compassion for the women whom they help to give birth, even at the risk of their lives. They are exemplars of *chesed shebetiferet*— they do acts of love born from compassion. Today is *Rosh Chodesh*, the new moon. The new moon is a symbol of rebirth — like the two midwives who help to birth the Hebrew slaves into a free people.

Hayom hamishah-asar yom, sheheim shnei shavuot veyom echad la'omer.
Today is fifteen days, two weeks and one day, of the Omer.

16. Devorah
Deborah the Judge (Judges 4-5)

Gevurah shebeTiferet   Judgment within Compassion

"Devorah, a prophetess and a bearer of light, judged Israel at that time. She sat under the palm tree of Devorah..." (Judges 4:4-5)

Deborah is the only woman judge to be mentioned in the book of Judges. *Gevurah* is her job — she sits under her palm tree and dispenses fair judgment to the tribes of Israel. Inspired by God, she appoints the warrior Barak to prepare for battle against the enemy general Sisera. Barak hedges, saying that he will not go to war unless Deborah goes with him. Deborah replies: "I will go with you, but the glory will not be yours (*tifartecha*, from *tiferet*) on the path you are walking, for God will deliver Sisera into the hands of a woman." The *tiferet* will instead go to Yael, the nomad woman who will kill Sisera with a tent peg while he sleeps in her tent.

When Deborah sings her song of triumph, she tells the story of the mother of Sisera, who waits behind her window for her son to come home, though her son is dead and will not return. The song is gloating, but also poignantly true to life. We might see Deborah's song of Sisera's mother as another instance of her judgment against the enemy, but it can also be viewed as an act of compassion to tell the story of the enemy's heartbreak.

Deborah embodies *gevurah shebetiferet* — judgment mixed with truth and compassion. She is a "mother of Israel," as her song says — one who can show empathy but also strength. We can imagine that these two qualities made Deborah a gifted judge. We imitate Devorah when we judge others in a fair way, allowing ourselves to see their point of view in addition to our own. Today is the second day of *Rosh Chodesh*, a day when the moon shines its light in darkness, as Devorah shone her light during a time of suffering.

Hayom shishah-asar yom, sheheim shnei shavuot ushnei yamim la'omer.
Today is sixteen days, two weeks and two days, of the Omer.

17. Chanah
Hannah (I Sam. 1-2)

Tiferet shebeTiferet   Compassion within Compassion

וְחַנָּה הִיא מְדַבֶּרֶת עַל־לִבָּהּ רַק שְׂפָתֶיהָ נָּעוֹת וְקוֹלָהּ לֹא יִשָּׁמֵעַ...

"Chanah was speaking in her heart; only her lips moved, but her voice could not be heard…" —I Samuel 1:13

Chanah, who lives in the time of the judges, has no children. Her husband Elimelekh loves her, but his other wife torments her because of her infertility. When Chanah goes with her family to the shrine at Shiloh as part of an annual pilgrimage, she prays for a son. She promises that if she becomes pregnant with a son she will dedicate him to the shrine so that he may serve God.

The priest Eli, observing her, thinks she is a drunkard and scolds her. Chanah protests that she is not drunk; she is a troubled woman who is speaking to God in her heart. Eli blesses her. Soon afterward, Chanah gives birth to a son, Samuel, whom she dedicates to the Tabernacle at Shiloh as soon as he is weaned. Every year from then on, Hannah makes a pilgrimage and brings Samuel a new coat that she has made.

Tiferet is the sefirah of the heart, Chanah speaks to God in her heart, telling God of her heart's desire to have a child. When confronted by someone who does not value her prayer because it is not public, she defends herself, knowing that God hears even the most private of prayers. Because of the words that Chanah speaks in her heart, God has compassion upon her. Chanah represents *tiferet shebetiferet*, the essence of compassion. We embody Hannah when we express the true desires of our heart, believing that our prayers are worthy of being answered.

Hayom shivah-asar yom, sheheim shnei shavuot ushloshah yamim la'omer.
Today is seventeen days, two weeks and three days, of the Omer.

18. Widow of a Prophet
II Kings 4:1-7

Netzach shebeTiferet   Endurance within Compassion

וְאִשָּׁה אַחַת מִנְּשֵׁי בְנֵי־הַנְּבִיאִים צָעֲקָה אֶל־אֱלִישָׁע לֵאמֹר עַבְדְּךָ אִישִׁי מֵת וְאַתָּה יָדַעְתָּ כִּי עַבְדְּךָ הָיָה יָרֵא אֶת־יְהוָה וְהַנֹּשֶׁה בָּא לָקַחַת אֶת־שְׁנֵי יְלָדַי לוֹ לַעֲבָדִים:

"A woman who was one of the wives of the disciples of the prophets cried out to Elisha, saying: 'Your servant my husband is dead, and you know that your servant feared God…'"
—II Kings 4:1

One Elisha story in the book of Kings tells of the widow of a certain "son of the prophets." According to a midrash, she is the wife of Obadiah, who saved the lives of many prophets of God when Jezebel, a foreign queen of Israel, sought to kill them. This widow comes to Elisha to tell him that a creditor is about to seize her children as slaves.

Elisha's first question to her is: "What do you have in the house?" She has nothing but a jug of oil. He tells her to borrow vessels from her neighbors, as many as she can get. Then she is to shut herself and her children in her home and pour the oil into these vessels until they are all filled. The widow does this, and miraculously, she has enough oil to fill all the vessels (this is a precursor to the Chanukah story)! She sells the oil, pays her bills, and she and her children live on the rest of the money.

Obadiah's widow has compassion on her young children and goes to the prophet Elisha in order to save them. He tells her that she cannot save her children unless she is both willing to ask for help from her neighbors, and willing to keep pouring as long as there is an empty vessel. The miracle of compassion (*tiferet*) that is done for her is done as a result of her own perseverance, her own quality of *netzach*. We best imitate Obadiah's widow when we are willing to work to bring about miracles.

Hayom shmonah-asar yom, sheheim shnei shavuot ve'arba'ah yamim la'omer.
Today is eighteen days, two weeks and four days, of the Omer.

19. Asnat
Genesis 41:45

Hod shebeTiferet   Beauty within the Heart

וַיִּקְרָא פַרְעֹה שֵׁם־יוֹסֵף צָפְנַת פַּעְנֵחַ וַיִּתֶּן־לוֹ אֶת־אָסְנַת בַּת־פּוֹטִי פֶרַע
כֹּהֵן אֹן לְאִשָּׁה וַיֵּצֵא יוֹסֵף עַל־אֶרֶץ מִצְרָיִם׃

"Pharaoh named Jospeh Tzafnat-Paneach, and he gave him Asnat daughter of Potiphera priest of On as a wife." —Genesis 41:45

Asnat, the wife of Joseph, is the daughter of the Egyptian priest of On. She marries Joseph and becomes the mother of Ephraim and Manasseh. Little is said about her, but her character has caught the imagination of commentators throughout history. There is an ancient Jewish novel called "Joseph and Asnat," telling her story.

According to one midrash, Asnat is Dinah's daughter (see day 11). She is conceived when Dinah is raped, and so Dinah's brothers want to kill the baby girl. Dinah's father Jacob puts an amulet around Asnat's neck that says "Holy to the Lord." The angel Gabriel takes her to Egypt and gives her to a childless couple — Potiphar and his wife. When Joseph is sold into slavery, he ends up in the house where Asnat has been raised. When Potiphar's wife accuses Joseph of rape, Asnat defends Joseph. In another midrash, while Egyptian women are throwing jewelry at Joseph because his beauty, Asnat throws Joseph her amulet, and he recognizes her secret identity.

When Joseph becomes Pharaoh's second-in-command, he asks for Asnat as his wife. Later, a midrash tells, Asnat asks Joseph to bring her two children, Ephraim and Manasseh, to receive Jacob's blessing. She is the originator of the ceremony we know today as "blessing the children." Asnat also has two granddaughters, She'erah and Maacah (I Chronicles 7:15 and 24). Through Asnat, blessing comes to daughters as well.

Although Asnat was born from a cruel act, she is "holy to God." Asnat is *hod shebetiferet* — beauty hidden in the heart. We are most like Asnat when we open to the secrets of our past and allow our blessings to reveal themselves.

Hayom tishah-asar yom, sheheim shnei shavuot vechamishah yamim la'omer.
Today is nineteen days, two weeks and five days, of the Omer.

20. Batya
Pharaoh's daughter (Exodus 2)

Yesod shebeTiferet   Connection Within Compassion

וַתֹּאמֶר אֲחֹתוֹ אֶל־בַּת־פַּרְעֹה הַאֵלֵךְ וְקָרָאתִי לָךְ אִשָּׁה מֵינֶקֶת מִן הָעִבְרִיֹּת וְתֵינִק לָךְ אֶת־הַיָּלֶד: וַתֹּאמֶר־לָהּ בַּת־פַּרְעֹה לֵכִי וַתֵּלֶךְ הָעַלְמָה וַתִּקְרָא אֶת־אֵם הַיָּלֶד:

"His sister said to Pharaoh's daughter, 'Shall I go and call for you a Hebrew nursing woman to nurse the child for you?' Pharaoh's daughter said to her: 'Go.'" —Exodus 2:7-8

The Pharaoh who enslaves the Hebrews is the epitome of all that is arbitrarily cruel. Yet his daughter, chooses to save a baby Hebrew that her own father has condemned. With the aid of the baby's sister Miriam, and the baby's mother Yocheved, who becomes the child's "wetnurse," Pharaoh's daughter rescues the child she finds in a reed basket and raises him as an Egyptian prince. (See artist's interpretation on page 26.) She names him Moses, "drawn out."

Without Pharaoh's daughter, whom the sages name Batya, "daughter of God," there would be no exodus and no redemption. She throws off whatever preconceived ideas her father's bigotry has given her about Hebrews and raises one of them as her own son. She becomes part of a female conspiracy to save life.

Batya is able to reach across lines of class and nationality and show compassion for others. Batya represents *yesod shebetiferet*, the connection of compassion, or the connectivity of the heart. We can follow in Batya's footsteps by reaching out to those who are unlike us and connecting with them in a kind and caring way.

This day is also *Yom ha'Atzma'ut*, Israeli Independence Day. Batya symbolizes all those who took tremendous risks to establish a homeland for the Jewish people, and also those who work across national and religious lines to create peace and justice for all those who dwell in the land of Israel.

Hayom esrim yom, sheheim shnei shavuot veshishah yamim la'omer.
Today is nineteen days, two weeks and six days, of the Omer.

21. The Shamaness of Ein-dor
The Witch of Endor (I Sam. 28)

Malchut shebeTiferet   The Dignity of Compassion

וַיֹּאמֶר שָׁאוּל לַעֲבָדָיו בַּקְּשׁוּ־לִי אֵשֶׁת בַּעֲלַת־אוֹב וְאֵלְכָה אֵלֶיהָ וְאֶדְרְשָׁה־בָּהּ וַיֹּאמְרוּ עֲבָדָיו אֵלָיו הִנֵּה אֵשֶׁת בַּעֲלַת־אוֹב בְּעֵין דּוֹר:

> "Saul said to his servants, 'Seek for me a woman who consults ancestor spirits, and I will go to her and seek an oracle through her.' His servants said to him: 'There is a woman who consults ancestor-spirits in Ein-dor.'" —I Samuel 28:7

King Saul's monarchy is collapsing. His once-loyal prophet, Samuel, tells him that God no longer wants him to be king. His rival, David, is gaining in power. Even Saul's own children support David as king of Israel. When Samuel dies, Saul faces war with Israel's enemies. Although Saul himself has banned witchcraft, he goes to a woman in *Ein Dor* (a name meaning "well of generations") who is known as a medium. Saul hopes Samuel will give him comfort and advice.

The woman of Endor, though at first she protests that witchcraft is punishable by death, calls up Samuel's spirit. Samuel's message is a cruel one — the next day, Saul and his sons will die in battle. Saul sinks onto the ground, miserable, as Samuel disappears. The witch encourages Saul to eat and lie down, and at last he is willing to take some food. The woman of Endor is one of the only people to show Saul compassion in the days before his death. An old woman whose profession is despised by the Israelite religion, she performs the work of midwiving Saul into death.

The witch of Endor, though she may be a controversial figure in an Omer calendar, is the ancestor of many mystics who speak with spirits, angels, and the prophet Elijah. Through her compassion, *tiferet*, she gives Saul dignity, *malkhut*, on the last night of his life. *Malkhut* also represents completeness. The witch of Endor reminds us that we need compassion in every stage of our lives: beginnings and endings.

Hayom echad ve'esrim yom, sheheim shlosha shavuot la'omer.
Today is three weeks of the Omer.

Fourth Week: *Netzach*

Endurance/Perseverance/Victory

Abraham's Servant meets Rebecca at the Well, Unknown mosaic artist,
Norman cathedral at Monreale, Sicily, c.1180
See page 38

22. Rebekah
Genesis 24-28

Chesed shebeNetzach   Love within Perseverance

וַיֹּאמְרוּ נִקְרָא לַנַּעֲרָ וְנִשְׁאֲלָה אֶת־פִּיהָ:

וַיִּקְרְאוּ לְרִבְקָה וַיֹּאמְרוּ אֵלֶיהָ הֲתֵלְכִי עִם־הָאִישׁ הַזֶּה וַתֹּאמֶר אֵלֵךְ:

"They said: 'We will call the girl and ask her what she says.'
They called for Rebekah and said to her: 'Will you go with this man?' She said: 'I will go.'"
—Genesis 24:57-58

Rebekah is going to the well to fetch water for her family when a stranger appears and asks her for water. Rebekah not only runs to quench the stranger's thirst, but offers to draw water for all of his camels as well! (See artist's interpretation on previous page.) This is *chesed shebenetzach* — Rebekah's endurance and zeal allows her to show generosity and love to others.

What Rebekah doesn't know is that this man is Abraham's servant and that he will ask her to accompany him back to Canaan to marry Isaac. Rebekah agrees to this request quickly and fearlessly. According to midrash, when Isaac brings Rebekah into the tent of his mother Sarah, Rebekah re-institutes all the sacred household practices of Sarah — candlelighting, bread-baking, and hospitality.

Rebekah's two sons, Jacob and Esau, are in conflict even in the womb. She inquires of God what to do, and God tells her that one day Esau will serve Jacob. In service to this prophecy, Rebekah tells Jacob to dress up as Esau in order to get Isaac's blessing. Then she sends him away to save him from Esau's anger, telling him to find a wife from among her relatives. She never sees him again.

Rebekah doesn't always act with chesed. She lies to her husband and desperately disappoints her eldest son. Yet Rebekah has chesed for the future, for the eternity that is *netzach* — she knows what must ultimately happen and acts to bring it about. We are most like Rebekah when we run to do chesed for the unnamed stranger and for the unknown future.

Hayom shneym ve'esrim yom, sheheim shlosha shavuot veyom echad la'omer.
Today is twenty-two days, three weeks and one day of the Omer.

23. Tziporah
Exodus 2:16-22, 4:24-26, 18:1-12

Gevurah shebeNetzach   Strength within Victory

וַתִּקַּח צִפֹּרָה צֹר וַתִּכְרֹת אֶת־עָרְלַת בְּנָהּ וַתַּגַּע לְרַגְלָיו וַתֹּאמֶר כִּי חֲתַן־דָּמִים אַתָּה לִי:

"Tziporah took a flint and cut off the foreskin of her son, and touched his legs with it, and said: 'You are a bridegroom of blood to me!'" —Exodus 4:25

Tziporah is the daughter of Yitro, the Midianite priest who takes Moses in after he flees Egypt. Her name means "bird." Moses marries Tziporah and she gives birth to two sons. After Moses receives the vision of the burning bush, he returns to Egypt. Tziporah and Moses' two sons accompany him.

At a night encampment, God attacks Moses and seeks to kill him. Tziporah takes a flint, cuts off her son's foreskin (it's not clear which son) and throws it at Moses' feet, saying: "A bridegroom of blood are you to me!" God leaves Moses alone, and Tziporah adds: "a bridegroom of blood, because of the circumcision."

Why does Tziporah act in this way? Rabbinic legend says that God is angry with Moses for failing to circumcise his son, and communicates this to Tziporah by causing Moses' sexual organs to swell! Others imagine that Tziporah, the daughter of a priest and perhaps a priestess herself, is offering the foreskin to God as a substitute sacrifice for Moses. Or, it may be that, since God has just decreed to Moses the killing of the first-born Egyptians, Moses' own status as the first-born of his adopted mother, an Egyptian princess, puts him in danger. Perhaps Tziporah uses the blood of the circumcision to create a transformed identity for Moses and his family.

Tziporah represents *netzach*, the ability to endure. In order to endure, she must practice *gevurah*—call on her power to cut, to separate, in order to protect life. We are most like Tziporah when we endure discomfort in order to achieve a lasting purpose.

Hayom shloshah ve'esrim yom, sheheim shlosha shavuot ushnei yamim la'omer. Today is twenty-three days, three weeks and two days of the Omer.

24. Hagar
Genesis 16, 21

Tiferet shebeNetzach   Compassion within Endurance

וַיִּמְצָאָהּ מַלְאַךְ יְהוָה עַל־עֵין הַמַּיִם בַּמִּדְבָּר עַל־הָעַיִן בְּדֶרֶךְ שׁוּר:
וַיֹּאמַר הָגָר שִׁפְחַת שָׂרַי אֵי־מִזֶּה בָאת וְאָנָה תֵלֵכִי...

"An angel of the Breath of Life found her by a spring of water in the wilderness...and said, 'Hagar, slave of Sarai, from where have you come, and where will you go...?'"
—Genesis 16:7-8

Hagar is the Egyptian maidservant of Sarai, wife of Abram. Sarai cannot conceive, so she gives Hagar to Abram as a concubine. Hagar becomes pregnant. Sarai, incensed at Hagar because she thinks Hagar is arrogant, abuses Hagar until she runs away.

An angel appears to Hagar and asks her: "Hagar, servant of Sarai, where are you coming from? Where are you going?" The angel tells Hagar to return and endure Sarai's harsh treatment, promising that she shall bear a son and call him Ishmael (God hears).

Hagar gives birth to Ishmael and he grows up. Sarai, now Sarah, conceives and gives birth to a son, Isaac. After Isaac's weaning-feast, Sarah sees Ishmael playing and demands that Hagar and Ishmael be sent away. Reluctantly, Abraham complies.

Hagar wanders in the desert, searching for water. When Ishmael is close to death, Hagar sits at a distance, unable to watch the death of her child. Again an angel appears, and tells Hagar that her son will become a great nation. God opens Hagar's eyes and she sees a well of water. She and Ishmael are saved. Ishmael grows up in the wilderness, becoming the father of many tribes.

Like all slaves, Hagar must struggle simply to survive. Her mistress chooses a sexual partner for her, abuses her, and wants to co-opt her child as well. Yet when Hagar suffers, God provides for her needs and promises her a great future. Hagar represents *tiferet shebenetzach*, the compassion within endurance, because Hagar's endurance allows her to discover God's angels of compassion. We are most like Hagar when we are able to open our eyes, even in the midst of our struggle, and see the beauty God has left lying near us.

Hayom arba'ah ve'esrim yom, sheheim shlosha shavuot veshlosha yamim la'omer.
Today is twenty-four days, three weeks and three days of the Omer.

25. Naamah
Noah's Wife; Genesis 4:22; 6:9-9:17

Netzach shebeNetzach   Persistence within Persistence

וַיָּבֹא נֹחַ וּבָנָיו וְאִשְׁתּוֹ וּנְשֵׁי־בָנָיו אִתּוֹ אֶל־הַתֵּבָה מִפְּנֵי מֵי הַמַּבּוּל:

"Noah, with his sons, his wife, and his sons' wives, came into the ark, because of the floodwaters." —Genesis 7:7

Not long after creation, God brings a great flood on the earth to destroy humankind. Only Noah and his family are saved. They must build an ark and endure many days of darkness while torrential waters cover the earth. At last, the dry ground reappears. God sets a rainbow in the sky as a sign that God will never destroy the earth again.

Noah's wife appears in the narrative, though she is not given a name. A woman named Naamah, daughter of Lamech and Tzilah, appears in Genesis 4:22. A midrash claims that this Naamah is Noah's wife, and that she is a graceful dancer and musician. Sandy Eisenberg Sasso, in a modern midrash called *A Prayer for The Earth: The Story of Naamah, Noah's Wife*, writes that while Noah is saving pairs of animals by taking them aboard the ark, Naamah is collecting every seed and bulb so that the plants of the earth will also be saved from the flood.

Naamah endures while the world is destroyed and rebuilt around her. She preserves life and enters a new world to raise future generations. Perhaps she brings seeds; perhaps she brings instruments. Either way, she holds the tools of life. She is the *netzach* in *netzach*, the deepest urge to endure. We are most like Naamah when we endure through the storm, when we collect seeds and shape tools to create the future.

Hayom chamishah ve'esrim yom, sheheim shlosha shavuot ve'arba'ah yamim la'omer. Today is twenty-five days, three weeks and four days of the Omer.

26. Nechushta
II Kings 24:8-17

Hod shebeNetzach   Surrender within Endurance

בֶּן־שְׁמֹנֶה עֶשְׂרֵה שָׁנָה יְהוֹיָכִין בְּמָלְכוֹ וּשְׁלֹשָׁה חֳדָשִׁים מָלַךְ בִּירוּשָׁלָ͏ִם וְשֵׁם אִמּוֹ נְחֻשְׁתָּא בַת־אֶלְנָתָן מִירוּשָׁלָ͏ִם: וַיֵּצֵא יְהוֹיָכִין מֶלֶךְ־יְהוּדָה עַל־מֶלֶךְ בָּבֶל הוּא וְאִמּוֹ וַעֲבָדָיו וְשָׂרָיו וְסָרִיסָיו וַיִּקַּח אֹתוֹ מֶלֶךְ בָּבֶל בִּשְׁנַת שְׁמֹנֶה לְמָלְכוֹ:

"Yehoyachin was eighteen when he became king... the name of his mother was Nechushta daughter of Elnatan of Jerusalem....King Yehoyachin of Judah went out to surrender to the king of Babylon, he and his mother and his servants and officers...."
—II Kings 24:8, 12

In ancient Israel, the position of the queen mother was an important political office. The queen mother advised the king, and may have had a religious function as well. When the names of the kings of Judah are listed, the names of the queen mothers always appear as well. When one of the last of the kings of Judah, Yehoyachin, is exiled to Babylon, his mother, Nechushta, daughter of Elnatan, is exiled with him.

Nechushta, "the bronze one," is related to the bronze serpents Moses uses to heal the Israelites in the wilderness (Num. 21: 4-9). When the people are struck by a plague of biting serpents, God tells Moses to make a bronze serpent (*nachash nechoshet*) and mount it on a staff. One who is bitten by a serpent can look at this bronze serpent and recover.

Nechushta, the queen mother of Israel, sees the looting of the Temple and the reduction of her culture to a mass of exiles, victims, and stolen goods. Yet her name is a reminder of the healing that Shekhinah can bring. A midrash about Nechushta claims that her doors were always open. Perhaps her doors remained open in exile so that like the bronze serpent, she could nourish and heal the other exiles.

In the end, Nechushta saw her son freed from prison—not an end to exile, but at least a sign of hope for the future. Nechushta is *hod shebenetzach*, the humility and grace we exhibit by enduring with hope. We are most like Nechushta when we find ways of nurturing healing in a broken world.

Hayom shishah ve'esrim yom, sheheim shlosha shavuot vechamishah yamim la'omer. Today is twenty-six days, three weeks and five days of the Omer.

27. Adah and Tzilah
Genesis 4:17-26

Yesod shebeNetzach   Connection within Endurance

וַיִּקַּח־לוֹ לֶמֶךְ שְׁתֵּי נָשִׁים שֵׁם הָאַחַת עָדָה וְשֵׁם הַשֵּׁנִית צִלָּה:

"Lamech took for himself two wives: the name of one was Adah, and the name of the other was Tzilah." —Genesis 4:19

Lamech, Cain's descendant, marries two women, Adah and Tzilah. According to one midrash, Lamech asks to have sexual intercourse with his wives. They reply: "The Flood [of Noah] is coming! If we listen to you, we will have children destined for the grave!" These prophetic women do not want to be fertile, since they have learned that the world will soon be destroyed.

Lamech asks Adam to judge between him and his wives. Adam asks Adah and Tzilah to return to their husband. The women reply: "Physician, heal your own limp!" In this midrash, Adam has been living separately from Eve since the death of Abel. So, Adam returns to Eve, and she gives birth to Seth, who will be the ancestor of Noah. Only then do Adah and Tzilah return to Lamech. Both have sons who invent the tools of civilization—herding, iron tools, and musical instruments. Tzilah also gives birth to Naamah, whom midrash claims is Noah's wife (see day 25).

Adah and Tzilah despair of the human potential to survive. What convinces them to try again is the support of community— Adam and Eve choose to invest in children. Because Adah and Tzilah make this commitment to life and help others to make it, the line of humanity can continue.

Yesod can mean sexual connection. One way we use *yesod*, sexuality, in the service of *netzach*, endurance, is by creating loving relationships and families. We are most like Adah and Tzilah when we take risks in order to make a future with those we love.

Hayom shivah ve'esrim yom, sheheim shlosha shavuot veshishah yamim la'omer. Today is twenty-seven days, three weeks and six days of the Omer.

28. Ritzpah
Saul's concubine; II Samuel 21:1-13

Malkhut shebeNetzach   Dignity within Endurance

וַתִּקַּח רִצְפָּה בַת־אַיָּה אֶת־הַשַּׂק וַתַּטֵּהוּ לָהּ אֶל־הַצּוּר מִתְּחִלַּת קָצִיר עַד נִתַּךְ־מַיִם עֲלֵיהֶם מִן־הַשָּׁמָיִם וְלֹא־נָתְנָה עוֹף הַשָּׁמַיִם לָנוּחַ עֲלֵיהֶם יוֹמָם וְאֶת־חַיַּת הַשָּׂדֶה לָיְלָה׃
וַיֻּגַּד לְדָוִד אֵת אֲשֶׁר־עָשְׂתָה רִצְפָּה בַת־אַיָּה פִּלֶגֶשׁ שָׁאוּל׃ ... וַיַּעַל מִשָּׁם אֶת־עַצְמוֹת שָׁאוּל וְאֶת־עַצְמוֹת יְהוֹנָתָן בְּנוֹ וַיַּאַסְפוּ אֶת־עַצְמוֹת הַמּוּקָעִים׃

"Then Ritzpah the daughter of Ayah took sackcloth and spread it on a rock for herself, and she stayed there from the beginning of the barley harvest. She did not let the birds of the sky settle on them by day or the wild beasts by night. David was told what Saul's concubine Ritzpah daughter of Ayah had done…and he gathered the bones of those who had been impaled…" —II Samuel 21:8-11, 13

While David is king over Israel, a famine comes to the land, and David inquires of God about it. God tells David that the land is being punished because the former king, Saul, put some Gibeonites to death. David asks the Gibeonites what he can do to appease them, and the Gibeonites reply that they want to kill seven of Saul's male relatives. David chooses the two sons of Ritzpah, a concubine of Saul, and five sons of Merav, Saul's elder daughter. He hands these men over to be impaled by the Gibeonites at the beginning of the barley harvest.

From the beginning of the barley harvest, Ritzpah stays with the bodies outdoors and does not let birds of prey land on them. When David is told what Ritzpah has done, he gathers up the bones of the men who have been impaled, and buries them in Saul's ancestral tomb in the territory of Benjamin. After David buries the bones, the famine ends.

Ritzpah uses her quality of *netzach*, her endurance and determination, in the service of dignity (*malkhut*). She is made in God's image. She deserves to mourn in a proper manner, and her sons deserve the decency of burial. By protecting the bodies of her children, she forces the authorities to pay attention to her cause. We are most like Ritzpah when we dignify the human spirit by refusing to be treated as less than human, even when we face power far greater than our own.

Hayom shmonah ve'esrim yom, sheheim arba'ah shavuot la'omer.
Today is twenty-seven days, three weeks and six days of the Omer.

Week Five: *Hod*

Glory/Receiving/Gratitude/Beauty

Das Opfer des Manoah, Willem Drost, 1641
See page 48

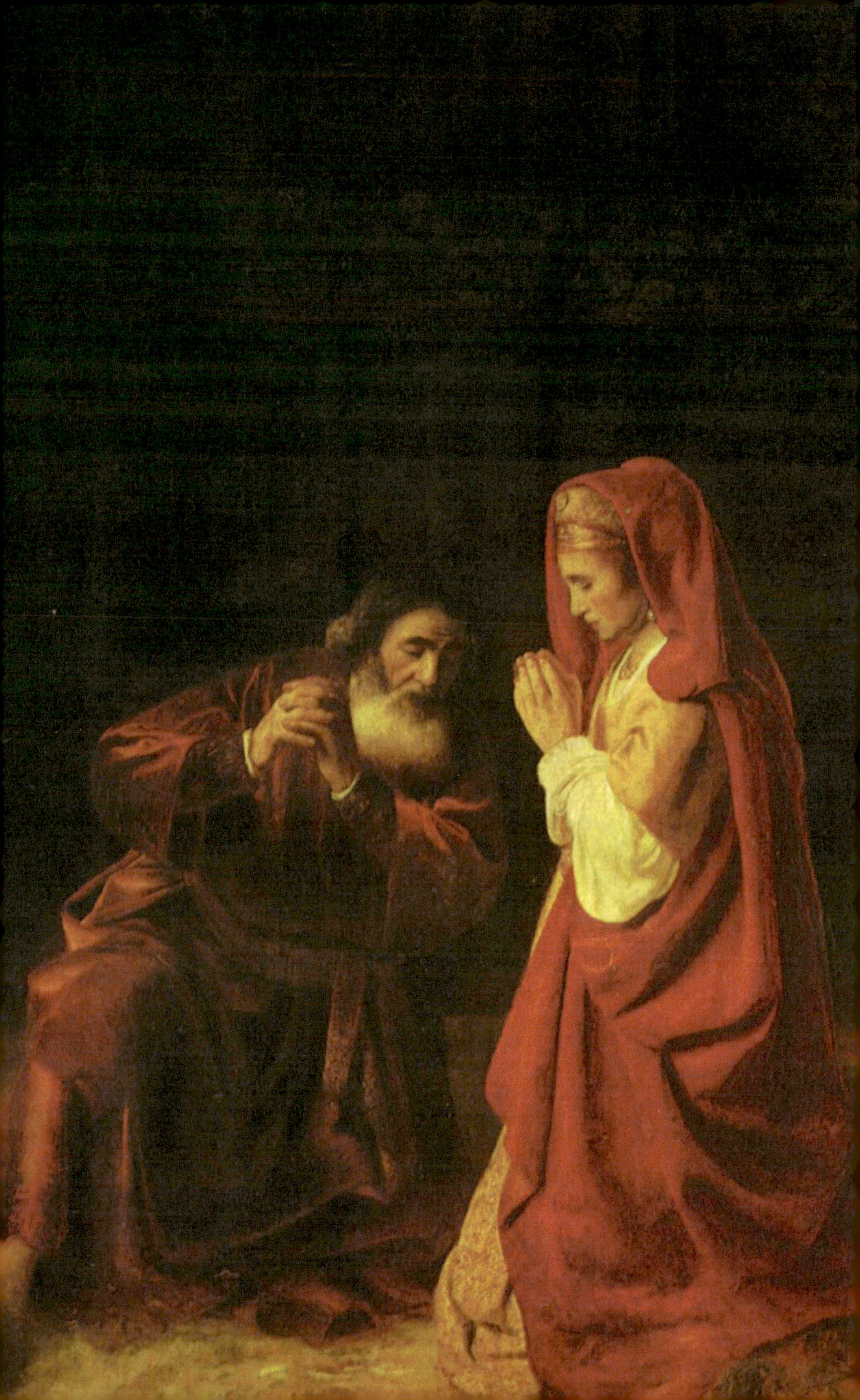

29. Hatzlelponit
Manoach's wife (Judges 13-14)

Chesed shebeHod   Generosity within Receiving

וַיִּשְׁמַע הָאֱלֹהִים בְּקוֹל מָנוֹחַ וַיָּבֹא מַלְאַךְ הָאֱלֹהִים עוֹד אֶל־הָאִשָּׁה וְהִיא יוֹשֶׁבֶת בַּשָּׂדֶה וּמָנוֹחַ אִישָׁהּ אֵין עִמָּהּ׃

"The angel of God came again to the woman, and she was sitting in the field, and Manoach her husband was not with her." —Judges 13:9

Manoach and his wife, who are childless, live in the time of the judges. Although the wife is nameless in the Bible, a midrash (drawing on I Chronicles 4:3) calls her Hatzlelponit. An angel appears to Hatzlelponit and tells her that she will bear a son. This child must be dedicated as a *nazir* (one who renounces wine, leaves his or her hair long, and stays away from dead bodies). His hair must never be cut. His mother must drink no wine during her pregnancy.

Hatzlelponit runs to tell her husband, and her husband prays to the angel to appear again. The angel does appear again, but only to Hatzlelponit while she is meditating in the field. The persistent woman runs to get her husband, but when Manoach huffs and puffs into the angel's presence, the angel tells him: "The woman must take care about all that I told her." When the angel disappears, Manoach is afraid that he will die, but Hatzelponit reasons: "Had God desired to kill us... he would not have shown us all these things." The child Hatzlelponit bears is Samson, who becomes a judge.

Because Hatzlelponit has the gift of acceptance (*hod*), she is able to understand God's generosity (*chesed*) when she receives it. Her husband is full of *gevurah*, of severity — he wants to know the rules, and he is afraid that God's presence will kill him. Hatzlelponit, however, is comfortable with the appearance of angels. She knows that the prophecy she has received is one of love. We are most like Hatzlelponit when we are able to take in the miracles of our lives with gratitude, and without fear. (See artist's interpretation on previous page.)

Hayom tishah ve'esrim yom, sheheim arba'ah shavuot veyom echad la'omer.
Today is twenty-nine days, four weeks and one day of the Omer.

30. Sarah
Genesis 12-23

Gevurah shebeHod   Strength within Glory

וַתֹּאמֶר שָׂרָה צְחֹק עָשָׂה לִי אֱלֹהִים כָּל־הַשֹּׁמֵעַ יִצְחַק־לִי׃

"Sarah said: God has made laughter for me; everyone who hears will laugh with me."
—Genesis 21:6

The Bible does not record that Sarai receives a call from God to go forth into a new land, but she does go, with her husband Abram, to the land of Canaan. Both Abram and Sarai receive new names— Abraham and Sarah. According to midrash, Sarah also has another name, *Iscah*, meaning "seer," because of the greatness of her prophetic spirit.

Sarah is barren. She offers her handmaid Hagar to Abraham as a concubine (see day 24), but God promises that the covenant with Abraham will be fulfilled through Sarah's womb. Three angels come to Sarah's tent and announce that she will become pregnant. She laughs, but she does become pregnant. She gives birth to a son whom she names Isaac, meaning "laughter."

Sarah's most difficult trial occurs when God orders Abraham to take her son Isaac to Mount Moriah and sacrifice him. In the Torah, Sarah has no role in this story, but Norma Rosen in *Biblical Women Unbound* imagines Sarah hauling a ram up the mountain for Abraham to use as a substitute. An ancient midrash suggests that Sarah only hears of what happens afterward, and the shock is so great that her soul leaves her. As she dies, she cries out, and in her cry the sound of the shofar is revealed for the first time.

Sarah's life is a wrestling match between the forces of *gevurah* and the power of *hod*, between the painful limitations of her life and the liberating prophecy she has received from God. We are like Sarah when we are immersed in grief and anger, and in delight and amazement — when we have knowledge of our painful human limits, and glimpses of God's glory.

Hayom shloshim yom, sheheim arba'ah shavuot ushnei yamim la'omer.
Today is thirty days, four weeks and two days of the Omer.

31. Elisheva
Exodus 6:23

Tiferet shebe'Hod   Compassion within Glory

וַיִּקַּח אַהֲרֹן אֶת־אֱלִישֶׁבַע בַּת־עַמִּינָדָב אֲחוֹת נַחְשׁוֹן לוֹ לְאִשָּׁה וַתֵּלֶד לוֹ אֶת־נָדָב וְאֶת־אֲבִיהוּא אֶת־אֶלְעָזָר וְאֶת־אִיתָמָר׃

> "Aaron took to wife Elisheva daughter of Aminadav, sister of Nachshon, and she bore him Nadav, Avihu, Elazar and Itamar." —Exodus 6:23

Elisheva is the sister of Nachshon son of Aminadav— the man who, according to legend jumps into the Sea of Reeds first! From the Bible, we only know that she is the wife of Aaron. Elisheva and Aaron have four sons. All *kohanim*, all hereditary members of the Israelite priesthood, are descended from her. The Talmud notes that Elisheva has five male relatives in prestigious positions — and claims she has "more joy than all the daughters of Israel!"

But who was she as an individual? What merit does Elisheva have that makes her a mother of priests? One legend about Elisheva says she was one of the midwives who saved Israelite children when Pharaoh ordered the Egyptians to kill them (see day 15). A modern midrash I wrote about Elisheva in the book *Sisters at Sinai: New Tales of Biblical Women* suggests that Elisheva was a midwife who saved the life of a first-born mother who gave birth to a first-born son on the night of the tenth plague. Elisheva confronted the angel of death and asked God to spare innocent lives in spite of the Divine decree. Because of her compassion, she merited the glory of the priesthood. So for me, Elisheva has become the symbol of *tiferet shebehod*, the compassion that resides in glory. We best exemplify the qualities of Elisheva when we seek to infuse our ritual and spiritual lives with compassion.

Hayom echad ushloshim yom, sheheim arba'ah shavuot ushloshah yamim la'omer. Today is thirty-one days, four weeks and three days of the Omer.

32. Naomi
Ruth 1-4

Netzach shebeHod — Endurance within Gratitude

וַתֹּאמַרְנָה הַנָּשִׁים אֶל־נָעֳמִי בָּרוּךְ יְהוָה אֲשֶׁר לֹא הִשְׁבִּית לָךְ גֹּאֵל הַיּוֹם וְיִקָּרֵא שְׁמוֹ בְּיִשְׂרָאֵל: וְהָיָה לָךְ לְמֵשִׁיב נֶפֶשׁ וּלְכַלְכֵּל אֶת־שֵׂיבָתֵךְ כִּי כַלָּתֵךְ אֲשֶׁר־אֲהֵבַתֶךְ יְלָדַתּוּ אֲשֶׁר־הִיא טוֹבָה לָךְ מִשִּׁבְעָה בָּנִים:

"The women said to Naomi, 'Blessed is the Breath of Life, who has not withheld a redeemer from you today… Your daughter-in-law who loves you bore him, and she is better to you than seven sons.'" —Ruth 4:14-15

When there is a famine in the land of Judah, Elimelekh, his wife Naomi, and their two sons leave Bethlehem and go to the land of Moab. While they are in Moab, Elimelekh dies, leaving Naomi a widow. Naomi's two sons marry Moabite women. Then the sons too die. Naomi hears that the famine in Judah is over, and decides to return home.

Naomi's two daughters-in-law, Ruth and Orpah, have no sons. Naomi encourages the two young women to go back to their mothers. Orpah kisses her mother-in-law and returns home, but Ruth clings to Naomi, saying: "Do not ask me to leave you… for where you go I will go…." And so Naomi allows Ruth to follow her back to Bethlehem.

When Naomi arrives in Bethlehem, she demands to be renamed Mara, bitterness. Yet Ruth works tirelessly for Naomi, gleaning in the fields. Finally, Naomi rouses herself to help Ruth, creating a plan whereby Ruth can convince Naomi's wealthy kinsman Boaz to marry the young Moabite. In the end, Ruth brings her son Oved home to Naomi. In spite of her afflictions, Ruth's love has brought Naomi a place in the world.

Hod is the sefirah of receiving. Naomi achieves *netzach*, endurance and victory, because even after so much has been taken from her, she is willing to accept Ruth's love. It is because Naomi can open her heart to receive the gift of Ruth's devotion that, in the end, she can open her arms to receive her unexpected adoptive grandson. We welcome the qualities of Naomi into our lives when we are willing to receive.

Hayom shnayim ushloshim yom, sheheim arba'ah shavuot ve'arba'ah yamim la'omer. Today is thirty-two days, four weeks and four days of the Omer.

33. Chuldah
Huldah the Prophetess (II Kings 22; II Chronicles 34:14-28)

Hod shebeHod   Receiving within Receiving

וַיֵּלֶךְ חִלְקִיָּהוּ הַכֹּהֵן וַאֲחִיקָם וְעַכְבּוֹר וְשָׁפָן וַעֲשָׂיָה אֶל־חֻלְדָּה הַנְּבִיאָה אֵשֶׁת | שַׁלֻּם בֶּן־תִּקְוָה בֶּן־חַרְחַס שֹׁמֵר הַבְּגָדִים וְהִיא יֹשֶׁבֶת בִּירוּשָׁלַם בַּמִּשְׁנֶה וַיְדַבְּרוּ אֵלֶיהָ׃

"The priest Chilkiahu…went to the prophetess Chuldah — the wife of Shallum son of Tikvah, keeper of the wardrobe — where she sat in the Jerusalem in the Mishneh, and they spoke to her." —II Kings 22:14

A righteous king of Judah, named Josiah, learns that the high priest has discovered a scroll in the Temple. Josiah does not know if the scroll is authentically the word of God. He asks a delegation of his royal officers to go to Chuldah, a prophetess who lives in Jerusalem, and find out from her whether he should govern according to the words of the scroll. Chuldah delivers her verdict: the scroll is authentic, and God plans to exile the people because they have disobeyed God's word. Josiah's lifetime will be peaceful, because he has humbled himself before God.

Chuldah, a woman, is not only a prophetess valued and respected by the king, but the first person in the Bible to canonize an uncertain text. (The scroll Chuldah reads is probably Deuteronomy.) The sages of the Talmud ask why the king consults a woman when there are other (male) prophets around. Yet it is clear that Chuldah is an important figure who begins a new kind of prophecy in Israel— the process of reading and interpreting sacred text. Chuldah represents *hod shebehod*, receiving within receiving, prophecy within prophecy, for her prophecy allows Israel to experience the prophetic voice in a new way.

The thirty-third day of the Omer is also Lag B'Omer, a minor holiday celebrated with bonfires. Lag B'Omer marks a day when Rabbi Akiva's students stopped dying of plague, and also the yahrtzeit (death date) of Shimon bar Yochai, traditionally named as the author of the Zohar. It is appropriate that Chuldah be remembered on a day that is a celebration of prophecy and Torah.

Hayom shloshah ushloshim yom, sheheim arba'ah shavuot vechamishah yamim la'omer. Today is thirty-three days, four weeks and five days of the Omer.

34. Avigayil
Abigail (I Samuel 25)

Yesod shebeHod   Connection within Beauty

וַיֹּאמֶר דָּוִד לַאֲבִיגַל בָּרוּךְ יְהוָה אֱלֹהֵי יִשְׂרָאֵל אֲשֶׁר שְׁלָחֵךְ הַיּוֹם הַזֶּה לִקְרָאתִי:

"David said to Abigail, 'Blessed be the Breath of Life, the God of Israel, who sent you this day to meet me! And blessed be your good sense, and blessed be you...'" —I Samuel 25:32

The young David, running away from King Saul, is earning his living by intimidating local farmers into providing him with bribes in return for the safety of their livestock. One wealthy and obnoxious landowner, Naval (meaning "fool") refuses to pay. David sets out with his men to kill Naval. But Naval's wife, Avigayil, is wise and beautiful, and her servants advise her that David has been gracious to them. Avigayil sets out to meet David, bringing with her bread, wine, sheep, raisins, figs, and other gifts.

When Avigayil meets David on the trail, she bows before him and delivers an eloquent speech asking David not to shed blood, for shedding blood will taint David's future kingdom. David, astonished, cries: "Blessed is the Eternal, God of Israel, who sent you to meet me this day!" David accepts Avigayil's gift and does not harm Naval. Naval hears of what has happened and dies of consternation. David takes Avigayil as a wife.

Hod represents beauty, and Avigayil uses the beauty of her speech to conciliate David. Within Avigayil's beautiful words lies her deep ability to connect. Avigayil is able to use *yesod*, connection, to open David's heart to her. In the end, their connection is so great that they marry one another. Because she predicts David's kingship, Avigayil becomes one of the seven women mentioned by the Talmud as prophetesses. It is appropriate that she symbolize *yesod shebehod* — the communciation of beauty. We are most like Avigayil when we use the beauty of our gifts to connect deeply with others.

Hayom arba'ah ushloshim yom, sheheim arba'ah shavuot veshishah yamim la'omer. Today is thirty-four days, four weeks and six days of the Omer.

35. Achsah
Joshua 15:13-19; Judges 1:10-15

Malkhut shebeHod   Sovereignty within Receiving

וַיֹּאמֶר כָּלֵב אֲשֶׁר־יַכֶּה אֶת־קִרְיַת־סֵפֶר וּלְכָדָהּ וְנָתַתִּי לוֹ אֶת־עַכְסָה בִתִּי לְאִשָּׁה:

"Caleb said: 'Whoever strikes and captures Kiriat-Sefer,
I will give him my daughter Achsah as a wife.'" —Joshua 15:16

The Bible tells Achsah's story twice, perhaps because a good story bears repeating. Achsah is the daughter of Caleb, one of the men who leads the conquest of the land of Canaan. Caleb promises his daughter Achsah to the man who can conquer the city of *Devir* (shrine), also called *Kiriat-sefer* (city of the book).

Caleb's cousin Otniel conquers the city, and Caleb gives Achsah to Otniel in marriage. As Achsah is leaving her father's home, she dismounts from her donkey and asks her father for a present — a land with springs of water. So her father gives her the area of Upper and Lower *Gulot* (springs) as a wedding gift.

This fairy tale of the princess who marries a hero becomes more interesting when one realizes that in midrash, Caleb is the husband of Miriam the prophetess — keeper of the miraculous well of the wilderness. While traditional midrash ignores the connection between Achsah and Miriam, it appears that Achsah is asking, not merely for territory, but for access to her mother's spiritual gift of water.

Achsah, although she is given away like an object, finds a way to reclaim her sense of *malkhut*, of individual sovereignty. She does this by asking for a gift — invoking the quality of *hod* or receptivity. Achsah asks springs of water from her father: perhaps the physical springs of a new land, the spiritual waters of Miriam's well, or even, as one midrash suggests, the wellsprings of Torah. We are most like Achsah when we ask for our physical, intellectual, and spiritual inheritance.

Hayom chamishah ushloshim yom, sheheim chamishah shavuot la'omer.
Today is thirty-five days, five weeks of the Omer.

Week Six: *Yesod*
Connection/Intimacy/Foundation

Judah and Tamar, School of Rembrandt, c.1640-1650
See page 64

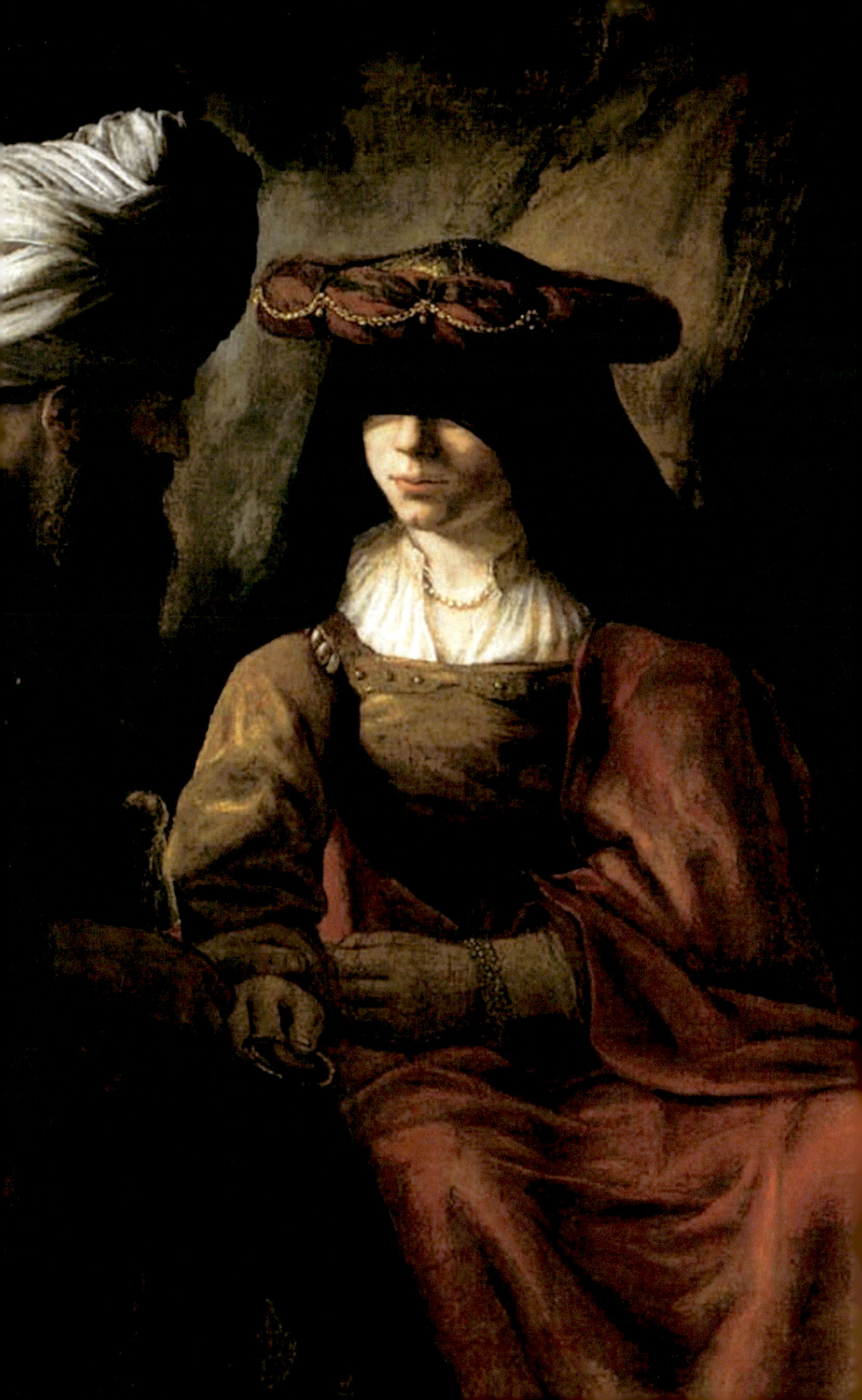

36. Rachav
Joshua 2, 6

Chesed shebeYesod   Generosity within Intimacy

וְאֶת־רָחָב הַזּוֹנָה וְאֶת־בֵּית אָבִיהָ וְאֶת־כָּל־אֲשֶׁר־לָהּ הֶחֱיָה יְהוֹשֻׁעַ וַתֵּשֶׁב בְּקֶרֶב יִשְׂרָאֵל עַד הַיּוֹם הַזֶּה כִּי הֶחְבִּיאָה אֶת־הַמַּלְאָכִים אֲשֶׁר־שָׁלַח יְהוֹשֻׁעַ לְרַגֵּל אֶת־יְרִיחוֹ:

"Joshua spared Rachav the prostitute and her family, and all that belonged to her, and she dwelled among the Israelites, as is still the case, for she hid the messengers that Joshua sent to spy on Jericho." —Joshua 6:25

When the Israelites enter the land of Canaan, they prepare to invade the city of Jericho. Two spies (tradition identifies them as Joshua and Caleb) enter the city and lodge with a prostitute named Rachav who lives in the wall of Jericho. The king of Jericho orders Rachav to produce the two men. Instead, she hides them under stalks of flax on her roof, and tells the king's guards that the men have left the city. Rachav lets the two men down the city wall by means of a red cord.

Rachav tells the two men that everyone in her city has heard about the miracles God has done for Israel, and everyone is afraid. She says to the men: "I have shown you kindness (*chesed*); now you show me and my family kindness (*chesed*)." The men promise that if she keeps their mission secret, they will save her and her family — all she has to do is display the red cord in her window. When Joshua attacks the city, he spares Rachav and her family. One midrash (Ruth Rabbah 2:1) says that she saved two hundred families in addition to her own. The midrash also claims that Joshua marries Rachav; they have five daughters and found a prophetic dynasty that includes the prophetess Chuldah (see day 33).

Rachav, a prostitute, deals in sexual intimacy (*yesod*) as a profession. She understands the power of connection. Rachav connects by giving chesed to two Israelite men who are in her power, and asking *chesed* from them. We invite Rachav into our lives when we turn enemies into friends by doing acts of *chesed*.

Hayom shishah ushloshim yom, sheheim chamishah shavuot veyom echad la'omer. Today is thirty-six days, five weeks and one day of the Omer.

37. Tamar
Daughter of David and Maacah (II Samuel 13)

Gevurah shebeYesod   The Strength within Connectivity

וַתֹּאמֶר לוֹ אַל־אָחִי אַל־תְּעַנֵּנִי כִּי לֹא־יֵעָשֶׂה כֵן בְּיִשְׂרָאֵל אַל־תַּעֲשֵׂה אֶת־הַנְּבָלָה הַזֹּאת:

"She said to him: 'No, brother. Don't rape me. Such things are not done in Israel. Don't do this terrible thing.'" —II Samuel 13:12

King David's eldest son Amnon is lovesick for his half-sister Tamar, a virgin princess. Amnon's slimy cousin Yonadav proposes a ruse: Amnon should pretend to be ill, and ask King David to send Tamar to make cakes for him in order to help him get well. Amnon does this, and David agrees to his odd request. While Tamar is cooking for Amnon, he seizes her.

Tamar pleads with Amnon, arguing that his behavior is wrong, and claims (perhaps in desperation) that David would give Tamar to Amnon as a wife if Amnon would ask for her in a decent way. Amnon does not listen to her; instead, he rapes her. Then, disgusted by her presence, he throws her out, though she protests that "to send me away is worse than the first wrong you committed." Tamar cries and tears her ornamented royal clothes — her coat of many colors, the same as Joseph's coat. Tamar goes to the home of her full brother Avshalom, who takes her in, but advises her to be silent. Two years later, Avshalom avenges his sister's rape by killing Amnon.

Tamar is vocal on her own behalf. She argues her case before her brother, and even after he has brutalized her she continues to condemn his behavior. Tamar argues for the potency of sexual limits, reminding Amnon that Israelites should not rape women. David's daughter Tamar represents *gevurah shebeyesod*, the need for boundaries of sexual connection. We are most like Tamar when we demand that our community never tolerate sexual violence, and insist that all people be free from sexual abuse.

Hayom shivah ushloshim yom, sheheim chamishah shavuot ushnei yamim la'omer. Today is thirty-seven days, five weeks and two days of the Omer.

38. Avishag
I Kings 1

Tiferet shebeYesod — Compassion within Intimacy

וַיְבַקְשׁוּ נַעֲרָה יָפָה בְּכֹל גְּבוּל יִשְׂרָאֵל וַיִּמְצְאוּ אֶת־אֲבִישַׁג הַשּׁוּנַמִּית וַיָּבִאוּ אֹתָהּ לַמֶּלֶךְ׃
וְהַנַּעֲרָה יָפָה עַד־מְאֹד וַתְּהִי לַמֶּלֶךְ סֹכֶנֶת וַתְּשָׁרְתֵהוּ וְהַמֶּלֶךְ לֹא יְדָעָהּ׃

"They found Avishag the Shunammite and brought her to the king. The girl was very beautiful, and she became an attendant to the king and served him, but the king was not sexually intimate with her." —I Kings 1:3-4

When King David is old, he is no longer able to have sex with women. He lies in his bed and shivers. His servants suggest that a young woman be brought to warm his bed. They begin a search for a beautiful girl, and find the "extraordinarily beautiful" Avishag the Shunammite. Avishag is brought to David. She serves the king, but they are not sexually intimate.

Avishag is a young woman appointed to be bedwarmer for an old and powerful man. No one seems to consult her about how she feels, though a number of Yiddish poems imagine her writing a melancholy letter to her mother, or promising the old, vain king that he still inspires fear in his subjects. Her fate seems dreary. Yet we also might see her as a powerful example of a caretaker.

In spite of Avishag's beauty, her role is not a sexual one. Avishag's experience is that of a helper to someone who is old and sick, who needs her presence to experience human warmth. Many of us at one time or another will have to care for someone who is young, elderly, ill, or impaired — to be intimate with their bodies and offer human connection to their souls. Like Avishag, caretakers must try achieve *tiferet shebeyesod* — compassion embodied in intimacy. We experience Avishag's presence in our lives when we provide for the physical needs of others with compassion and gentleness.

Hayom shmonah ushloshim yom, sheheim chamishah shavuot ushloshah yamim la'omer. Today is thirty-eight days, five weeks and three days of the Omer.

39. Mahlah, Noa, Choglah, Milcah, and Tirtzah
The Daughters of Tzelafchad (Num. 27:1-11, 36; Jos. 17:3-6)

Netzach shebeYesod   The Victory within Connection

וַיֹּאמֶר יְהוָה אֶל־מֹשֶׁה לֵּאמֹר: כֵּן בְּנוֹת צְלָפְחָד דֹּבְרֹת נָתֹן תִּתֵּן לָהֶם אֲחֻזַּת נַחֲלָה בְּתוֹךְ אֲחֵי אֲבִיהֶם וְהַעֲבַרְתָּ אֶת־נַחֲלַת אֲבִיהֶן לָהֶן:

"The Breath of Life said to Moses: 'The daughters of Tzelafchad speak correctly. Give them a land-holding among their father's brothers, and give their father's share to them.'"
—Numbers 27: 6-7

While the Israelites are wandering in the wilderness, Moses assigns the males of each tribe a portion of land in Canaan. Tzelafchad, a man of the tribe of Manasseh, has died, leaving behind five daughters: Machlah, Tirtzah, Choglah, Milcah, and Noa. These five brave women appear in front of Moses to ask for an inheritance of land in their father's name. "Let not our father's name be lost to his family just because he had no son!" they argue. Moses takes the matter before God, and God replies: "The daughters of Tzelafchad have spoken rightly — give them an inheritance among their father's kinsmen." But there is a catch — the daughters can only marry within their tribe, so that their land will not pass to sons who belong to a different clan.

Living in their time and place, the daughters of Tzelafchad cannot argue for equality of sons and daughters. Even after their case is heard, daughters will not inherit alongside their brothers. What Machlah, Tirtzah, Choglah, Milcah, and Noa can and do achieve is an acknowledgement that daughters have a connection to their family, to their past, and to their land. That connection should not be discounted simply because they are women. The daughters of Tzelafchad ask that God, Moses, and the community recognize their love and commitment. They are exemplars of *netzach shebeyesod* — the victory that arises out of connection. We act according to the example of the daughters of Tzelafchad when we organize to speak up about injustice, when we sustain our family's traditions, and when we demand that others take our values and commitments seriously.

Hayom tishah ushloshim yom, sheheim chamishah shavuot ve'arba'ah yamim la'omer. Today is thirty-nine days, five weeks and four days of the Omer.

40. The Queen of Sheba
Bilqis (I Kings 10:1-12)

Hod shebeYesod   Receptivity within Communication

וּמַלְכַּת־שְׁבָא שֹׁמַעַת אֶת־שֵׁמַע שְׁלֹמֹה לְשֵׁם יְהוָה וַתָּבֹא לְנַסֹּתוֹ בְּחִידוֹת׃

"The Queen of Sheba heard reports of Solomon by means of God's name, and she came to test him with riddles." —I Kings 10:1

The Queen of Sheba is a mysterious figure who appears in Solomon's court in order to test his wisdom. She comes from a far land in Africa to Jerusalem, bringing camels, spices, gold, and jewels, and asks Solomon riddles. The Muslim tradition calls her Bilqis. Solomon shows the Queen his great edifices, the luxury of his court, the manners of his officials. Bilqis asks the king many questions, and there is nothing he does not know. Bilqis is delighted by his wisdom. In some legends, she and Solomon become lovers.

Some Jewish legends see the Queen of Sheba as a demoness with hairy legs, whom Solomon defeats by cunning. Yet the Queen of Sheba can teach us about curiosity and peaceful cultural exchange. She hears of something extraordinary she has not seen — a truly wise king — and she sets out to discover whether what she has heard is true. She too is wise, yet she is unashamed to say that she finds great wisdom in Solomon. She brings gifts from her own land and exchanges them for the gifts that Solomon gives her: "Solomon gave the Queen of Sheba all that she desired and asked for." Through this exchange she gains material wealth, intellectual wisdom — and perhaps a friend.

The Queen of Sheba represents *hod shebeyesod* — the receptivity that comes from deep connection. She is a model for explorers, adventurers, and peacemakers. We are most like her when we are curious about the world, and when we reach out to discover lands and people we have never known.

Hayom arba'im yom, sheheim chamishah shavuot vechamishah yamim la'omer. Today is forty days, five weeks and five days of the Omer.

41. Shulamit
Song of Songs 1-8

Yesod shebe Yesod   The Connection within Intimacy

שׁוּבִי שׁוּבִי הַשּׁוּלַמִּית שׁוּבִי שׁוּבִי וְנֶחֱזֶה־בָּךְ מַה־תֶּחֱזוּ בַּשּׁוּלַמִּית כִּמְחֹלַת הַמַּחֲנָיִם:

"Again, again, O Shulamit! Again, again, let us look at you!" "What visions will you see in the Shulamite, in the dance of Mahanaim?" —Song of Songs 6:13

The Song of Songs is a love poem full of lush language and snatches of narrative — a maiden in a garden longing for her shepherd lover, a man praising a woman with dark eyes like doves. Rabbi Akiva called the Song of Songs "the Holy of Holies" and believed it was an allegory of God and Israel. Others see the Song as a secular love poem, or a ritual of sacred marriage between feminine and masculine divine. The woman of the Song of Songs is named Shulamit. She may come from a place called Shulem, or perhaps her name is like her character — peaceful, whole, complete. Shulamit is also similar to Shulmanitu —"she of the peace-offering," a name of the goddess Ishtar.

Shulamit goes out searching for the one she loves. "Let us go into the vineyards" she cries. "Let us see if the vine has flowered, if the blossoms have opened and the pomegranates are budding. There I will give my love to you." Her lover answers her in a similarly rich and eager tone. Unlike most of the Bible, where sexuality is subject to rules and harsh realities, the sensuality of the Song of Songs is free and gentle, based in loving relationship. It is not violent but playful, not hierarchical but poetic.

Shulamit teaches us about the power of deep intimacy — sexual and spiritual, with humans and with nature. She is *yesod shebeyesod*, perfect connection. We welcome her into our gardens when we experience our intimate relationships as loving, equal, and fluid — as part of the song of everything.

Hayom echad ve'arba'im yom, sheheim chamishah shavuot ushishah yamim la'omer. Today is forty-one days, five weeks and six days of the Omer.

42. Tamar
Genesis 38

Malchut shebeYesod   Majesty within Connection

וַתָּסַר בִּגְדֵי אַלְמְנוּתָהּ מֵעָלֶיהָ וַתְּכַס בַּצָּעִיף וַתִּתְעַלָּף וַתֵּשֶׁב בְּפֶתַח עֵינַיִם אֲשֶׁר עַל־דֶּרֶךְ תִּמְנָתָה כִּי רָאֲתָה כִּי־גָדַל שֵׁלָה וְהִוא לֹא־נִתְּנָה לוֹ לְאִשָּׁה:

"She put away her widow's clothes, covered herself with a veil, wrapped herself, and sat at the gate of Enayim with is on the road to Timnah, for she saw that Shelah had grown up, but she had not been given to him as a wife." —Genesis 38:14

Judah, after helping to sell Joseph into Egypt, takes a Canaanite wife and has three sons. When his eldest son is old enough, Judah finds him a wife — Tamar. Er is displeasing to God, and he dies. Tamar has no child, so the rule of levirate marriage applies. In levirate marriage, the brother of a deceased man marries the deceased man's childless widow, in order to provide his brother with substitute offspring. Judah marries his second son, Onan, to Tamar, but Onan spills his seed on the ground, not wanting to provide heirs for his brother. God causes Onan to die too.

Judah tells Tamar to go home to her family until the third son, Shelah, is grown up. Shelah grows up but Tamar is not given to him in marriage. She remains a childless widow, bound to Judah's family. Taking matters into her own hands, Tamar veils herself and dresses as a prostitute. She goes out to sit by the city gate, and Judah comes to her. (See artist's interpretation on page 57.)

Tamar becomes pregnant. When Judah finds out, he wants to have Tamar burned, but Tamar proves he is the father. Judah acknowledges his wrong, saying: "She is more righteous than I." Tamar gives birth to twins, Peretz and Zerach. Peretz becomes the ancestor of King David.

The connection Tamar forms with Judah restores fairness, gives Tamar a chance at a full life, and gives Judah an opportunity to repent. Tamar also gives rise to the kings of Israel. Tamar represents *malkhut shebeyesod* — the majesty that arises out of intimate connection. We open to Tamar's influence when we form relationships that bring lasting fullness to others and to ourselves.

Hayom shnayim ve'arba'im yom, sheheim shishah shavuot la'omer.
Today is forty-two days, six weeks of the Omer.

Week Seven: *Malkhut*
Majesty/Dignity/Presence/Earth

Ruth and Boaz, Janet Shafner, 1999
See page 68

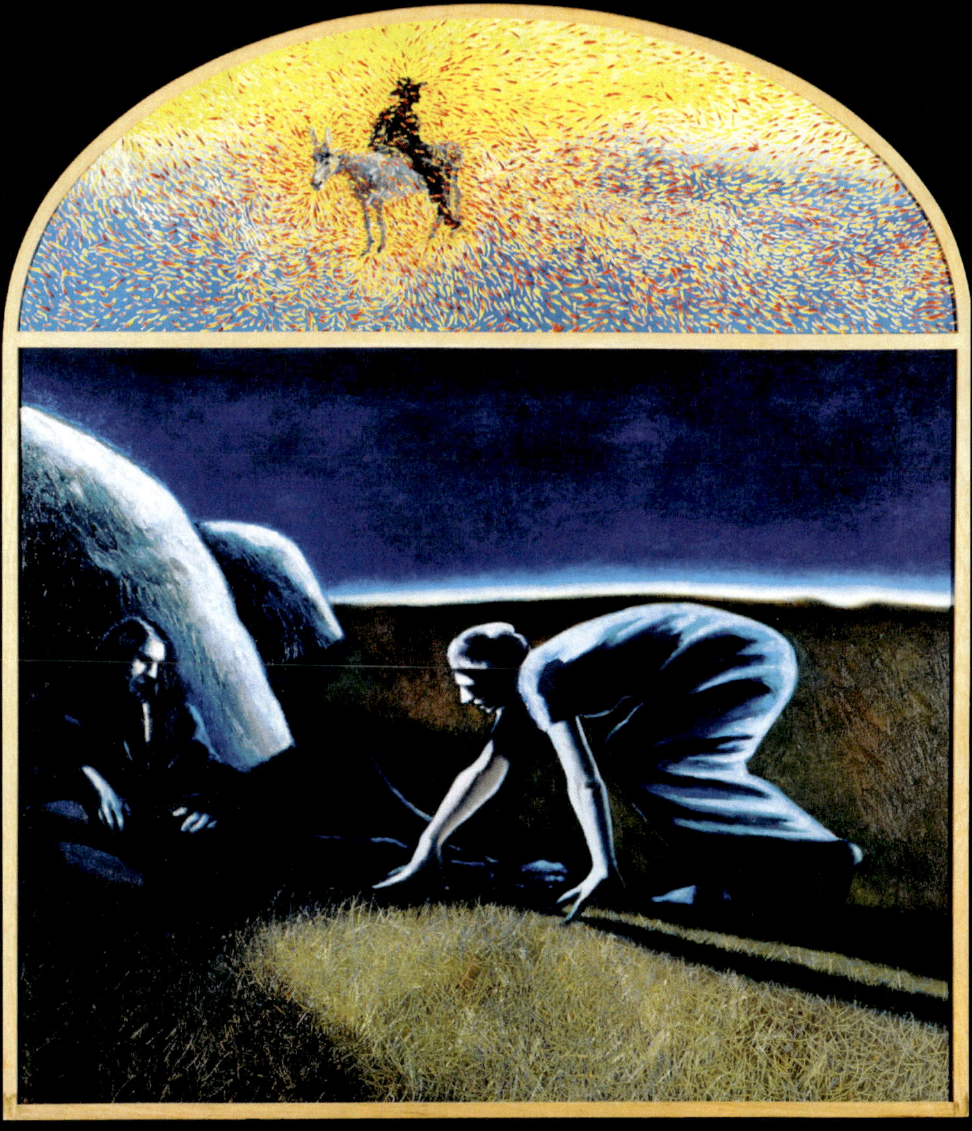

43. Ruth
Ruth 1-4

Chesed shebeMalkhut   Love within Majesty

וַתֹּאמֶר רוּת הַמּוֹאֲבִיָּה אֶל־נָעֳמִי אֵלְכָה־נָּא הַשָּׂדֶה וַאֲלַקֳטָה בַשִּׁבֳּלִים אַחַר אֲשֶׁר אֶמְצָא־חֵן בְּעֵינָיו וַתֹּאמֶר לָהּ לְכִי בִתִּי׃

"Ruth the Moabite said to Naomi: 'May I go to the field and glean among the ears of grain, behind someone who may show me kindness?' And she said to her: 'Go, daughter.'"
—Ruth 2:2

Ruth, a Moabite, marries the son of Naomi, an Israelite who has come to Moab because of a famine in the land of Judah. When Naomi's sons and husband die, Naomi wants to leave Moab, but Ruth refuses to return to her family. The two walk on together toward Bethlehem, where they will be poor and without protection.

Ruth works in the field, gleaning barley that harvesters have dropped. Boaz, a wealthy landowner and kinsman of Naomi, speaks kindly to her, offering her food and a place to rest. Boaz tells Ruth that he admires her because he has heard of the good things she has done for Naomi. Naomi conceives the plan that Ruth and Boaz should marry.

Naomi tells Ruth to dress in fine clothes and lie down on the threshing floor where Boaz is sleeping. (See artist's interpretation on the previous page.) When Boaz awakes, Ruth asks him to act as a "redeeming kinsman" and perform a levirate marriage with her (see day 32). Boaz is stunned that this young woman wants to wed him, and tells her: "Your latest *chesed* is even greater than your first." Boaz arranges a meeting of the town elders and obtains permission to marry Ruth. She gives birth to a son, Oved, the grandfather of King David.

A midrash tells us that the book of Ruth was written to show how great is the reward for doing acts of chesed. Ruth is *chesed shebemalkhut* — the love inside the kingdom, the love that flows through all things. We are most like Ruth when we do acts of lovingkindness for the sake of increasing God's presence in the world.

The day of *chesed shebemalkhut* begins the week prior to Shavuot. Ruth's story is read on Shavuot because of her dedication to the Jewish people.

Hayom shloshah ve'arba'im yom, sheheim shishah shavuot veyom echad la'omer. Today is forty-three days, six weeks and one day, of the Omer.

44. Michal
I Samuel 18:20-29; 19:8-17; II Samuel 3:12-16, 6

Gevurah shebeMalkhut   Severity within Majesty

וְהָיָה אֲרוֹן יְהוָה בָּא עִיר דָּוִד וּמִיכַל בַּת־שָׁאוּל נִשְׁקְפָה ׀ בְּעַד הַחַלּוֹן וַתֵּרֶא אֶת־הַמֶּלֶךְ דָּוִד מְפַזֵּז וּמְכַרְכֵּר לִפְנֵי יְהוָה וַתִּבֶז לוֹ בְּלִבָּהּ׃

"As the Ark of the Breath of Life came into the City of David, Michal daughter of Saul looked out of the window and saw David leaping and whirling before the Breath of Life, and she despised him in her heart." —II Samuel 6:16

Michal is the daughter of King Saul. The book of Samuel says of her that she loves David. This is one of only three times in the Bible that women are said to love anyone. King Saul promises Michal to his rival David as a wife, thinking that his daughter will help him keep an eye on David. Instead, Michal helps David escape her father, using the ruse of putting a stone idol in David's bed. David runs off to the wilderness, abandoning his wife, and Saul forces Michal to marry another man.

When Saul dies and David becomes king, David demands Michal as part of the nation's peace settlement. Michal's husband Paltiel follows her, weeping. Michal says nothing, and she does not weep. Yet she has feelings about what has happened. When David dances and whirls before the Ark as it is brought into Jerusalem, Michal criticizes him, saying: "Didn't the king do himself honor today, exposing himself in the sight of his subjects' slavegirls?!" David shames her by reminding her of her father's defeat. The text records that to her dying day Michal had no children— either because she was barren or because David refused to have sex with her.

Michal shows courage in defending her husband from her father, and later shows considerable strength in standing up to him when she does not like his behavior, though he is more powerful than she. She is *gevurah shebemalkhut*: the strength of majesty, or the limitation of power. We are most like her when we are willing to question the behavior of the powerful.

Hayom arba'ah ve'arba'im yom, sheheim shishah shavuot ushnei yamim la'omer. Today is forty-four days, six weeks and two days, of the Omer.

45. Rachel
Genesis 29-32, Jeremiah 31:15-17

Tiferet shebeMalkhut   Compassion within Majesty

כֹּה ׀ אָמַר יְהוָה קוֹל בְּרָמָה נִשְׁמָע נְהִי בְּכִי תַמְרוּרִים רָחֵל מְבַכָּה עַל־בָּנֶיהָ מֵאֲנָה לְהִנָּחֵם עַל־בָּנֶיהָ כִּי אֵינֶנּוּ׃ כֹּה ׀ אָמַר יְהוָה מִנְעִי קוֹלֵךְ מִבֶּכִי וְעֵינַיִךְ מִדִּמְעָה כִּי יֵשׁ שָׂכָר לִפְעֻלָּתֵךְ נְאֻם־יְהוָה וְשָׁבוּ מֵאֶרֶץ אוֹיֵב׃

> "A voice is heard in Ramah, lamentation and bitter weeping, Rachel weeping for her children.... Thus said the Breath of Life, 'Stop your voice from sobbing and your eyes from tears, for there is a reward for your labor, says God, and they shall return from enemy country, and there is hope for your future — the children will return to their land.'"
> —Jeremiah 31:15-16

Jacob serves his unscrupulous uncle Laban for seven years in order to marry Rachel, his beloved. Laban pulls a switch and disguises Rachel's older sister Leah as Rachel at the wedding. Jacob is willing to serve Laban another seven years so he can have Rachel as well.

Leah is prolific and Rachel is infertile. This causes Rachel great anguish. She pleads with her husband for children. She offers her handmaid Bilhah to Jacob as a childbearing concubine. She even offers Leah a night with Jacob in return for mandrakes, an herbal remedy for infertility. Finally, Rachel gives birth to a son, Joseph. Later, on the road near Bethlehem, Rachel dies in childbirth with her second son Benjamin. Many pilgrims today go to her tomb to ask for fertility.

Rachel is known for her powers of intercession with God. In one legend, God is angry with the Israelites for worshipping other gods, and swears that they will never return from exile. The patriarchs and prophets plead with God, but God refuses to listen. Then Rachel reminds God that when Leah married Jacob and lay with him, Rachel hid under the bed, speaking in Rachel's voice, so that Leah would not be discovered and shamed. She overcame her jealousy for her flesh-and-blood sister. Should not God overcome any jealousy as well — since the other gods are not even real? God relents and promises to redeem the exiles.

The kabbalah teaches that Rachel represents *malkhut*, the sefirah of the Shekhinah. Rachel exemplifies the compassion of the Shekhinah for her people — *tiferet shebemalkhut*. We are most like Rachel when we model in our own lives the way we want to see all people treated.

Hayom hamishah ve'arba'im yom, sheheim shishah shavuot ushloshah yamim la'omer. Today is forty-five days, six weeks and three days, of the Omer.

46. Yehosheva
II Kings 11

Netzach shebeMalkhut — Victory within Sovereignty

וַתִּקַּח יְהוֹשֶׁבַע בַּת־הַמֶּלֶךְ־יוֹרָם אֲחוֹת אֲחַזְיָהוּ אֶת־יוֹאָשׁ בֶּן־אֲחַזְיָה וַתִּגְנֹב אֹתוֹ מִתּוֹךְ בְּנֵי־הַמֶּלֶךְ [הַמֻּמָתִים] (הַמּוּמָתִים ק) אֹתוֹ וְאֶת־מֵינִקְתּוֹ בַּחֲדַר הַמִּטּוֹת וַיַּסְתִּרוּ אֹתוֹ מִפְּנֵי עֲתַלְיָהוּ וְלֹא הוּמָת׃

"Yehosheva, daughter of King Yoram and sister of Ahaziah, took Yoash son of Ahaziah, stole him from among the princes who were being murdered, and hid him and his wetnurse in a bedroom. They kept him hidden away from Atalyah, so he would not be killed." —II Kings 11:2

Yehosheva is a woman with an infamous heritage. She is granddaughter of Jezebel, the queen of Israel who orders the prophets of God killed. She is the daughter of Atalya: a queen mother of Israel who, when her son the king dies, orders all the males of the royal house killed, even her own grandsons, so that she can assume the throne.

Yehosheva defies her mother and acts to save one of the king's sons. While Atalya reigns, Yehosheva hides away young Yoash and his nurse in a secret room in the Temple. Six years later, Yehosheva's husband, the high priest Yehoyada, reveals Yoash to the Israelites. He anoints Yoash as king, and has Atalya executed. From one point of view, the story is disturbing, as it depicts powerful women like Atalya and Jezebel as conscienceless and unjust, while good and righteous women support the kingship of men. Yet even if we read the story as it stands, Yehosheva, a woman, takes center stage as a moral personality.

Yehosheva has a choice: she can be loyal to her mother, and perhaps become queen herself, or she can act against her mother's callous and unethical acts. Yehosheva's decision to hide a threatened child and uphold his kingship shows that her commitment is to righteousness and not only to political power. Yehosheva represents the victory, *netzach*, of *malkhut*, God's sovereignty. We are most like Yehosheva when we do not idealize our own power, but rather use our strength to increase good in the world.

Hayom shishah ve'arba'im yom, sheheim shishah shavuot ve'arba'ah yamim la'omer. Today is forty-six days, six weeks and four days, of the Omer.

47. Esther
Esther 1-10

Hod shebeMalkhut   Surrender within Sovereignty

וַיְהִי | בַּיּוֹם הַשְּׁלִישִׁי וַתִּלְבַּשׁ אֶסְתֵּר מַלְכוּת וַתַּעֲמֹד בַּחֲצַר בֵּית־הַמֶּלֶךְ הַפְּנִימִית נֹכַח בֵּית הַמֶּלֶךְ וְהַמֶּלֶךְ יוֹשֵׁב עַל־כִּסֵּא מַלְכוּתוֹ בְּבֵית הַמַּלְכוּת נֹכַח פֶּתַח הַבָּיִת:

"On the third day, Esther put on royal robes, and stood in the innermost courtyard of the palace, facing the king's house, and the king was sitting on his royal throne in the throne room, facing the door of the palace." —Esther 5:1

Esther is a Jewish girl growing up in Persia with her uncle Mordechai. The king's officials select her to enter the harem of King Ahasuerus after he divorces his wife Vashti (see day 9). Esther is very beautiful, and the king makes her his new queen. At her uncle's request, Esther keeps her Jewish identity secret. Meanwhile, the king's advisor, Haman, has decided to exterminate the Jews. The king agrees to Haman's decree, and Haman sets a date for his genocidal order to be carried out.

Mordechai asks Esther to help. At first she refuses, saying that if she enters the king's throne room without being summoned, the king will kill her. Mordechai tells her that she too will perish if the Jews are killed, and: "Who knows if it is for this that you have risen to royal estate?" Esther agrees to go in to the king and plead for her people's safety.

After numerous courtly dinners, Esther presents her case before the king. The king grants Esther's petition, and orders Haman hung on the gallows he intended for Esther's uncle Mordechai. The Jews declare a holiday, Purim. Esther writes down the story in a scroll and sends it to all the Jews.

When Esther stands in the throne room before the king, she is wearing royal robes — literally, she is wearing *malkhut*. Esther achieves dignity through her willingness to take action to save her people. She accepts that her position must be used for the benefit of others. She is an exemplar of *hod shebemalkhut* — the surrender that arises from sovereignty. We are most like her when we ask ourselves how we can use our own privilege to serve God and our fellow beings.

Hayom shivah ve'arba'im yom, sheheim shishah shavuot vechamishah yamim la'omer. Today is forty-seven days, six weeks and five days, of the Omer.

48. Batsheva
II Sam. 11, I Kings 1-2

Yesod shebeMalkhut   Connection within Sovereignty

וַתָּבֹא בַת־שֶׁבַע אֶל־הַמֶּלֶךְ שְׁלֹמֹה לְדַבֶּר־לוֹ עַל־אֲדֹנִיָּהוּ וַיָּקָם הַמֶּלֶךְ לִקְרָאתָהּ וַיִּשְׁתַּחוּ
לָהּ וַיֵּשֶׁב עַל־כִּסְאוֹ וַיָּשֶׂם כִּסֵּא לְאֵם הַמֶּלֶךְ וַתֵּשֶׁב לִימִינוֹ:

"Batsheva went to King Solomon… The king arose to greet her, and bowed to her, and then he sat on his throne, and had a throne placed for the queen mother, and she sat at his right hand." —I Kings 2:19

King David, bored because he hasn't gone out to battle in a while, sees Batsheva bathing on a rooftop and demands that she be brought to him, even though she is married to one of David's officers. When Batsheva finds herself pregnant, David's solution is to invite Batsheva's husband Uriah home from the front for a night in his wife's bed. Uriah refuses. David tells his general to put Uriah in the front lines where he will be killed. When Uriah dies in battle, David marries Batsheva.

Nathan the prophet tells David that God will punish him for his crime. When Batsheva's son is born, the child falls ill and then dies. David mourns for his son and attempts to comfort Batsheva, but Batsheva remains a mystery. Does she hate David? Love him? How does she feel about the murder of her husband?

What is clear is that Batsheva gets her political feet very quickly. She gives birth to another son, Solomon, and David promises that this son will be king. When David dies, Batsheva is the first woman to occupy the position of *gevirah*, queen mother (see day 26). She sits on a throne by her son Solomon.

Batsheva finds herself in a tragic situation as a young woman. She grows into a wise, mature, and regal personage. She begins as *yesod shebemalkhut*, sexual connection within royalty, in one sense — the beautiful and fertile woman who creates David's dynasty. She becomes *yesod shebemalkhut* in a different sense: the foundation of the kingdom, a wielder of regal power. We are most like Batsheva when we age gracefully, learning the lessons of our experience.

Hayom shmonah ve'arba'im yom, sheheim shishah shavuot veshishah yamim la'omer. Today is forty-eight days, six weeks and six days, of the Omer.

49. Shekhinah

Malkhut shebeMalkhut   Majesty within Majesty

ר' שמעון הוה יתיב ולעי באורייתא בליליא דכלה אתחברת בבעלה, דתנינן כל אינון חברייא דבני היכלא דכלה אצטריכו בההיא ליליא דכלה אזדמנת למהוי ליומא אחרא גו חופה בבעלה, למהוי עמה כל ההוא ליליא ולמחדי עמה בתקונהא דאיהי אתתקנת, למלעי באורייתא מתורה לנביאים ומנביאים לכתובים ובמדרשות דקראי וברזי דחכמתא, בגין דאלין אינון תיקונין דילה ותכשיטהא. ואיהי ועולמתהא עאלת וקיימת על רישיהון ואתתקנת בהו וחדת בהו כל ההוא ליליא, וליומא אחרא לא עאלת לחופה אלא בהדייהו, ואלין אקרון בני חופתא.

> "R. Shimon was sitting and studying the Torah during the night when the bride was to be joined to her husband. For we have been taught that all the members of the bridal palace, during the night preceding the Shekhinah's espousals, must rejoice with her in her preparations for the great day: to study all branches of the Torah… for these represent her adornments. The bride with her bridesmaids comes up and remains with them, adorning herself at their hands and rejoicing with them all that night, and on the following day She enters the chuppah in their company." —Zohar I, 8a

The forty-ninth day of the Omer is the day before Shavuot, the festival of the wheat harvest and the giving of the Torah. On Shavuot, Shekhinah descends on Mount Sinai to grant revelation to the people. The Zohar teaches that we should stay up all night on Shavuot studying Torah, because our insights are like jewels for the bride Shekhinah as she prepares for her wedding with the transcendent Holy One.

In the kabbalah, *malkhut*, royalty or majesty, is the Shekhinah, who is called queen, princess, crown, and other royal names. These royal images are meant to convey both the Shekhinah's power and her involvement in the welfare of those who dwell in Her world. On this day of *malkhut shebemalkhut*, we reflect on the power of divinity acting within us and within the world around us. We prepare to receive the covenant of Torah, which is also a manifestation of God's presence.

In the Jewish understanding, this is also the final day of the grain harvest. On this day we pray that we will use the grain we have gleaned from God's storehouse for good, that we may nourish ourselves and do lovingkindness for one another. Blessed is the One who has kept us in life and sustained us and enabled us to reach this season.

Hayom tishah ve'arba'im yom, sheheim shivah shavuot la'omer.
Today is forty-nine days, seven weeks, of the Omer.

Index of Images

Cover
Ruth in the Fields, Merle Hugues, 1876

Week One: *Chesed*
Misés e Jocabed, Pedro Américo, 1884

Week Two: *Gevurah*
Lot's Wife, Janet Shafner, 1996

Week Three: *Tiferet*
The Finding of Moses, Sir Lawrence Alma-Tadema, 1904

Week Four: *Netzach*
Abraham's Servant Meets Rebecca at the Well, Unknown mosaic artist, Norman cathedral at Monreale, Sicily, c.1180

Week Five: *Hod*
Das Opfer des Manoah, Willem Drost, 1641

Week Six: *Yesod*
Judah and Tamar, School of Rembrandt, c.1640-1650

Week Seven: *Malchut*
Ruth and Boaz, Janet Shafner, 1999

ABOUT THE ART: Sholom Shafner, husband of midrashic artist Janet Shafner (may her memory be a blessing), gave permission for her two paintings "Lot's Wife" and "Ruth and Boaz" to be part of this Omer Calendar. Her paintings also appear at janetshafner.com. All other paintings appear according to "fair use" copyright laws.

Index of Names

A
Aaron 4, 9, 11, 50
Abraham 4, 20, 38, 40, 49
Abram. *See* Abraham
Achsah 54
Adah 43
Adam 18, 43
Ahasuerus 19, 72
Aminadav 50
Amnon 59
Asnat 21, 32
Atalya 71
Avigayil 53
Avishag 60

B
Batsheva 73
Batya 33
Bat Yiftach 23
Bilqis 62

C
Cain 18
Caleb 54
Chanah 30
Chava 18
Choglah 61
Chuldah 52

D
Daughters of Tzelafchad 61
David 53
Deborah. *See* Devorah
Devorah 29
Dinah 21, 32

E
Eli 30
Elijah 34
Elimelekh 51
Elisha 10, 14
Elisheva 50

Ephraim 32
Er 64
Esau 38
Esther 19, 72
Eve 18

H
Hagar 40
Haman 72
Hannah 30
Hatzlelponit 48
Huldah 52

I
Idit 20
Ishmael 40

J
Jacob 13
Jephthah. *See* Bat Yiftach
Jephthah's daughter 23
Jethro. *See* Yitro
Jezebel 71
Job's daughters 22
Joseph 32, 64
Joshua 58
Josiah 52
Judah 64

K
Keren-happuch 22
Ketziah 22

L
Laban 24, 70
Lamech 43
Leah 21, 24, 70
Lot 20
Lot's wife 20

M

Maacah 32, 59
Mahlah 61
Manasseh 32
Manoach 48
Manoach's Wife 48
Merav 44
Michal 69
Milcah 61
Miriam 3, 9, 10, 11, 28, 33, 54
Mordechai 72
Moses 9

N

Naamah 41, 43
Naaman 10
Nachshon 50
Naomi 51
Nathan 73
Nechushta 42
Noa 61
Noah 41

O

Onan 64
Orpah 51
Otniel 54

P

Peretz 64
Pharaoh 28
Pharaoh's daughter 33
Puah 28

Q

Queen of Sheba 62

R

Rachav 58
Rachel 4, 24, 70
Rebekah 24, 38
Reuven 24
Ritzpah 44
Ruth 3, 51, 58, 66, 68, 75

S

Samuel 34
Sarah 38, 40, 49
Sarai. *See* Sarah
Saul 34
Saul's concubine 44
Serach bat Asher 13
Seth 18
Shamaness of Ein-dor 34
She'erah 32
Shekhinah 3, 4, 8, 42, 70, 74, 79
Shifrah 28
Shulamit 63
The Shunnamite 14
Solomon 12

T

Tamar (daughter of David) 59
Tamar (Er's wife) 64
Tirtzah 61
Tzilah 43
Tziporah 39

U

Uriah 73

V

Vashti 19, 72

W

Witch of Endor 34

Y

Yehosheva 71
Yemima 22
Yiftach. *See* Bat Yiftach
Yitro 39
Yoash 71
Yocheved 11, 28, 33

Z

Zerach 64

About the Author

Rabbi Jill Hammer, PhD, is the Director of Spiritual Education at the Academy for Jewish Religion (www.ajrsem.org) and the co-founder of the Kohenet Institute, a program in Jewish women's spiritual leadership (www.kohenet.org). Rabbi Hammer is a midrashist, a ritualist, and the author of two books: *Sisters at Sinai: New Tales of Biblical Women* (Jewish Publication Society, 2001) and *The Jewish Book of Days: A Companion for All Seasons* (Jewish Publication Society, 2006). She has been exploring the stories of biblical women since her college days and continues to discover new layers of their legends and lives.

Her literary writing and academic work has been published in journals and newspapers such as *Zeek Magazine, Lilith Magazine, The Journal of Feminist Studies in Religion, Natural Bridge, The Torah: A Women's Commentary, Nashim,* and *The Forward*, and on-line at ritualwell.org, myjewishlearning.org, and other websites. Rabbi Hammer was ordained at the Jewish Theological Seminary in 2001 and holds a doctorate in social psychology from the University of Connecticut. She received a BA at Brandeis University. She lives in Manhattan with her partner Shoshana Jedwab and her daughter Raya Leela.

About the Designer

Shir Yaakov Feit is the Creative and Musical Director of Romemu, New York City's Center of Judaism for Body, Mind, and Spirit. He is a singer, songwriter and performer, and the co-founder of the band Darshan. His solo albums include are *Shir, Zeh* and *Az*. He lives near Manhattan's last natural forest with his partner Emily and daughter Ivy Lila.

Jill Hammer and Shir Yaakov Feit have been collaborating since 2004, when they co-created Tel Shemesh, a website celebrating earth-based Judaism. In 2006, when Hammer co-founded the Kohenet Institute with Holly Taya Shere, Feit became Kohenet's art designer and webmaster, and designed the Kohenet prayerbook. They also collaborate in prayer and ritual contexts at the Isabella Freedman Jewish Retreat Center and at Romemu in New York City. This Omer calendar is a natural outgrowth of their love and appreciation for one another's work.

Rabbi Hammer thanks Rabbi Zalman Schachter-Shalomi, whose work she consulted in choosing women for the *sefirot*, along with the Zohar and the writings of the kabbalist Menachem Azarya of Fano.